MEDJUGORJE
UNDER SIEGE

Reserve Book

MEDJUGORJE
UNDER SIEGE

David Manuel

PARACLETE PRESS
Orleans, Massachusetts

With deepest appreciation, I would like to acknowledge—

Father Svet, for encouraging this project. . .
Jozo Kraljevic, for his interpreting and his contemporary overview. . .
Doctor Professor Slavko Kovacic, lecturer in Church History at the
  College of Theology in Split, for his patient guidance through the
  intricacies of Croatian history. . .
Father Martin Shannon, for his editorial insight. . .
Bishop Henry Hill for his wisdom regarding the Orthodox Church. . .
Janet and Bob Edmonson for their transcribing. . .
Publisher Lillian Miao, for caring enough to say the very worst, and
  for keeping this project on its impossible schedule. . .
The staff of Paraclete Press, for their prayers and sacrifice. . .
And my wife Barbara, for putting up with the impossible.

1st Printing, March, 1992
2nd Printing, September, 1992

ISBN: 1-55725-052-9
Printed in the United States of America

To the visionaries and villagers,
priests and nuns
of Medjugorje,
whose hearts reflect
the heart of Jesus
on the Way of the Cross—

Blessed are the meek,
for they shall inherit the earth.

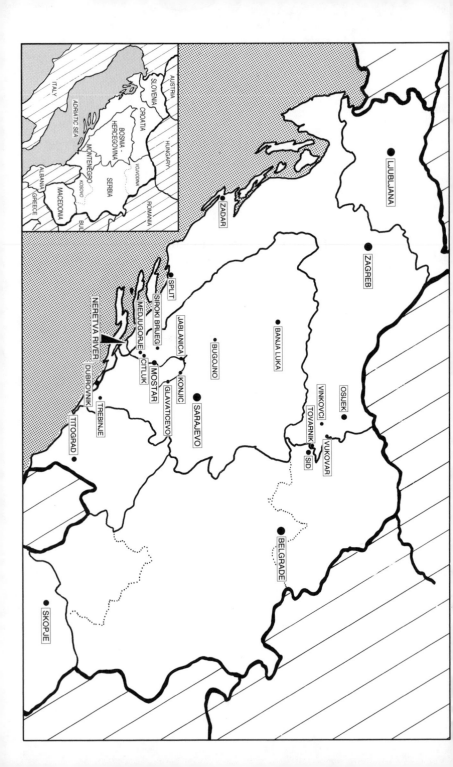

Table of Contents

Part III   The Present

Part IV   The Future

Foreword

I was in England, halfway through a two-week speaking tour, when David Manuel called, asking if I would do the foreword to his new book. As usual, it was a last-second request, and as usual it was needed immediately.

Having worked with David as my editor on *Medjugorje: The Message* and *Letters from Medjugorje,* I was accustomed to last-minute deadlines and requests. It is a seemingly unfixable part of a writer's modus operandi we share. Within forty-eight hours, the manuscript was delivered—just in time for a long, six-hour train ride to my next speaking engagement. As customarily happens with things concerning Medjugorje, it was perfect timing.

Hours appeared to become minutes, as I sat fascinated by the clarity and conciseness of *Medjugorje Under Siege;* it is a unique mix of up-to-the-second happenings and critical historical events, leading to the present war drama surrounding Medjugorje and its Croatian people. Having co-authored an historical spiritual book on America's founding days of early democracy, David's skill as an historical writer is obvious. Adding to the fascination is the fact that David, a Protestant, has been able to delicately balance objective history and fact of the region with the deep-seated emotions and unshakable faith in God of its predominately Catholic population.

This is no easy task—especially for a writer with a strong Protestant background. But David has found the good "fruit" of Medjugorje's apparitions personally. Now, in *Medjugorje Under Siege,* he has adroitly captured the need to virtually live the messages in order to bring peace to the area as requested so often in the past ten years of daily apparitions by the mother of Jesus.

It is obvious from this book that while ever the professional writer and accomplished historian, David Manuel's heart and soul have been captured by the spiritually powerful events of this little village called Medjugorje.

—Wayne Weible

I

The Crisis

1

Krizevac

Friday, the 13th of December—It was peaceful atop Mt. Krizevac that afternoon, twelve days before Christmas. There was not much warmth in the hazy sunlight of three o'clock, but the wind was down. Soon the sun would be down as well; already the shadow of the mountain stretched half-way to the twin spires of St. James in the valley below. On the horizon to the north, the peaks of the mountains beyond the Neretva River were all white with snow. At its eastern extremity loomed Mt. Velez—the distant brooding presence in every Medjugorje landscape.

Other than Father Svet's editor, there was only one other person on the summit that afternoon—an old man in a black cap, sitting at the base of the cross. An hour before, a thousand people had congregated here. At the invitation of Father Slavko, they had joined him and the visionary Mirjana in praying the Stations of the Cross up the mountain. Many of them were villagers, but there were also many who had come from Citluk and Ljubuski, and as far away as Mostar. They had come to pray for peace, as the *Gospa* had requested.

Ten years before, when the Blessed Mother had first appeared to the six young people of Medjugorje, she had asked them—and everyone else—to pray, fast, convert, repent, and forgive. Thereafter, whenever she called for prayer, she specifically urged people to pray for peace. It may have puzzled them, at first; it didn't any longer.

With war ravaging the neighboring republic of Croatia and threatening to ignite "neutral" Bosnia-Hercegovina at any moment, her monthly messages to the world had been getting increasingly urgent. Last month's, the shortest ever, consisted of three words: *Pray, pray, pray!*

Now, a thousand people had joined Mirjana and Father Slavko to do just that. Some were quite old, and for them the ascent up the steep rocky path had been extremely difficult. But as always, others had readily helped them, and as always, it was well worth the effort. They prayed and softly sang *Ave Maria,* and descended happy and at peace in their hearts. And an hour later, the fragrance of that peace seemed to linger in the air on the mountaintop.

A few months before, Mt. Krizevac would have been teeming with pilgrims from all over the world, praying the rosary, taking pictures of friends in front of the cross, finding a quiet place to commune with God. Then on June 26th, all that ended.

Yugoslavia was comprised of six individual republics. The largest, to the east, was Serbia, flanked by Hungary, Rumania, and Bulgaria. The southernmost was Macedonia, whose name reflected its affinity with Greece, just below it. The smallest was Montenegro, just above Albania on the Adriatic coast. Above it, in the middle of Yugoslavia, was Bosnia-Hercegovina, surrounded by Serbia to the east and Croatia to the north and west. Just above Croatia, and below Austria, was Slovenia.

In 1948, when Tito set up Communist Yugoslavia, he included in the constitution a clause whereby the six republics which had "voluntarily" joined the federation, were free to leave at any time they chose—never dreaming that such a day might actually come to pass. In each republic the Communist party was in absolute control, which it would never relinquish.

But in 1989, with Communism caving in everywhere else, the Communist parties in four of the republics, faced with the increasing domination of the Communist party of Serbia and its perpetual ally Montenegro, forced a national referendum—the first totally free election in Yugoslavia, since 1918. They were well aware that the people might reject Communism entirely, but even that was preferable to being amalgamated into the Communist equivalent of Greater Serbia.

The people did reject Communism resoundingly—in all but Serbia and Montenegro. There, though it now called itself Socialism, nothing had changed; a rose was still a rose. Immediately the two northernmost republics, Slovenia and Croatia, started negotiating for their departure. But since they had the strongest economies and contributed roughly half the national income, there were elements which were reluctant to see them go. These introduced one delaying tactic after another, until finally in June of '91, the two northernmost republics declared their independence anyway. At which point, the new shared (but Communist-directed) federal government authorized the Communist-controlled federal army to prevent them.

Suddenly, war in Yugoslavia was the lead story on the evening news in America. There on our television screens in vivid color, were hastily-roused Slovenian and Croatian militias, many armed with World War II rifles, trying to defend their homeland against the planes, tanks, and heavy artillery of the third largest land army in Europe.

In Belgrade, the U.S. Embassy told all American pilgrims in Medjugorje to go home at once, and in Washington the State Department strongly advised all travel agencies planning pilgrimages to Medjugorje to cancel said plans forthwith. Other countries did the same; within a week, the remote village in the mountains of Hercegovina, which had been visited by more than a million pilgrims annually, had become a ghost town.

When the editor had arrived in Medjugorje on July 6, en route to Konjic to go over the final draft of *Pilgrimage* with its author, Father Svetozar Kraljevic, he found the village deserted. The vast stone plaza in front of St. James church, normally teeming with pilgrims on a Saturday noon, was empty. No one sat in the new cafes that lined the main street; no one frequented the new shops. In fact, the only people to be seen were half a dozen forlorn guides, hanging out at the information kiosk. Inside the church, which in other times would be at least half full between services, there was one person praying.

But it was peaceful here, he exclaimed to Father Slavko Barbaric, the visionaries' spiritual director, when he called on him at the rectory. The war was confined to Croatia's eastern province Slavonia, several hundred miles away. He had rented a car in Dubrovnik with no problem, although it was strange being one of only 20 guests at the Hotel Belvedere the night before; it usually had a long waiting list for its 400 beds at this time of year. But other than a couple of checkpoints on the drive up, he had seen nothing unusual—no soldiers at all, let alone troop movements.

The brown-robed friar smiled sadly. "Tell your friends, when you go home. Perhaps the pilgrims will return."

But during his week with Father Svet, the fighting around Vukovar had worsened, and he barely got out of Dubrovnik on the last Pan Am flight.

Gradually pilgrims from America did start coming back, despite the State Department's position. And then, on September 20th, the federal army fully mobilized, attacking all along the eastern border of Croatia, striking south at to the coast and down to Dubrovnik, and simultaneously thrusting up the coast from Montenegro. Anticipating the likelihood that the conflict would soon engulf Bosnia-Hercegovina (the federal army was very good at anticipating), they had invited Serbian reservists and civilian irregulars to join it in Mostar, the capital of the province of Hercegovina. The largest concentration of Croatians was in this region; in the event of hostilities, the greatest resistance would be encountered here.

On September 20th, several thousand of these paramilitary troops arrived, investing the hills around Mostar and setting up observation posts on their summits. With this new development, the U.S. Embassy in Belgrade called Medjugorje and told all American citizens to leave the country immediately, requesting their passport numbers. The U.N. sanctions against Yugoslavia were about to go into effect, which meant the borders could be sealed within 48 hours.

Panic swept through the small contingent of American pilgrims. Frantically they tried to arrange departure by air out of Sarajevo, or even by ferry across the Adriatic. When they phoned the embassy to give their passport numbers, they reported hearing random gunfire in the hills. Someone atop Mt. Krizevac was certain that they had seen several thousand men massing on the other side of the mountain for an assault on the village, with more joining them all the time. Someone else reported that all the men of the village had been called away to man barricades defending the approaches to Citluk and Medjugorje. The embassy duly passed on these reports to Washington, and the State Department included them in its strongest advisory yet: no more Americans should go to Yugoslavia, and travel agencies should not even *think* of planning any more pilgrimages. In America, among the more than a million pilgrims who had been to Medjugorje, had their lives profoundly changed as a result, and had a deep affection for that place, apprehension was already running high. They had been watching the evening news with dread, hoping that for once the war in Croatia would *not* be a lead story. No news was truly good news. But night after night, there it was—beautiful Dubrovnik being mercilessly shelled; tragic Vukovar, already so devastated that the continuing bombardment was doing little more than bouncing rubble, with rows of bloated corpses. And in the back of everyone's mind was the thought: How long before this horror touched Medjugorje?

The State Department's alarming advisory seemed to lend credibility to the hysterical "bulletins" that some misguided pilgrim in Medjugorje had begun faxing across the Atlantic. And each person hearing a wild rumor could not help embellishing it or just adding the emotional freight of their own genuine concern. As a result, the fear was amplified exponentially.

By the morning of the 21st, practically everyone who cared about Medjugorje had heard—always from purportedly reliable sources—one or more of the following: Podbrdo had been bombed! St. James was in ruins! Women and children were being machine-gunned in the streets of the village! Father Jozo had been killed! Father Slavko had been taken hostage!

To combat this firestorm of panic-fueled rumor, a few friends of Medjugorje who had long maintained professional contact with the village, now tried desperately to get calls through. But telephone communication, difficult enough under ordinary circumstances, was now almost impossible. For once, those high-tech phones with repeat auto-dialing capability came in handy; at last, contact was established.

The rumors proved to be just that. It was true that several thousand Serbian reservists and civilian irregulars had arrived in the area, but they were still on the other side of the Neretva River, twenty kilometers away. It was true that the men of the village had organized a five-man patrol which walked the countryside at night, but each man drew the duty only twice a month, and their main activity was making sure that villagers observed the blackout. It was true that random gunfire was being heard in nearby hills, but as often as not it was from Croatians, taking target practice or letting off steam. Father Slavko and Father Svet, contacted separately by their editors, used the same expression to summarize the situation in Medjugorje: "Tense but calm."

In America, much of the next two days was spent stamping out the fire that the rumors had started, tracing the rumors back to their sources, and urging those who had circulated them to act more responsibly in the future. Given the incendiary climate in Hercegovina, it was all too possible that one day there might be emergency news of the gravest nature to report. In that event, it was best to leave the dissemination to the Medjugorje centers. Anyone in the network should exercise maximum care not to pass on anything that had not been checked out with a proven reliable source, and not to attach their own concern.

In the ensuing months, the war news grew even darker. Dubrovnik was battered and starving, its hotels in ruins. On the eastern front, Vukovar had fallen, and the city of Osijek was now receiving the same treatment. Fully a third of Croatia was now under Serbian control. And now reports of atrocities, documented on videotape, were coming to the West. The details were so grotesque, it seemed inconceivable that modern man could inflict such things on other men. Satanic was the adjective most often employed (even by those who did not believe in Satan).

With no pilgrims going to Medjugorje, there were no first-hand reports coming home, and as always happened, rumors were quick to fill the void. Paraclete Press, publisher of a number of books on Medjugorje, began receiving increasing queries, as to the safety of the visionaries, villagers, and priests. The editor was now in regular contact with Father Svet, and the news was getting progressively worse.

2

"Come and see"

Father Svet was angry. He was in his new assignment, as spiritual director of the eighty-five sisters at the convent in Potoci, a little village just north of Mostar, on the Neretva, and his mood could be easily discerned, despite the fading and echoing of the trans-Atlantic connection. (His editor was surprised; this was one of the most imperturbable men he had ever encountered.) "Last night," he exclaimed, "very late, a man called here. He would not identify himself to the sister who answered, and only said: 'We know you have munitions there.' When she protested, he replied, 'Well, we shall see,' and hung up." The Franciscan paused. "You can imagine what state that put the sisters in!"

What did he do? "We prayed. They knew that Satan was prowling, and that their fear only made him happier."

He calmed down then, but he was still gravely concerned. It was the first week of December, and it had turned cold. Since their arrival in September, the Serbian civilian irregulars—they called themselves "freedom fighters";

11

Father Svet called them terrorists—had been living in tents. With the arrival of winter, they were anxious to get indoors; the warm convent beds could accommodate half a platoon.

The allusion to hidden war materiel followed their standard operating procedure. Their pretext for destroying more than 270 churches, monasteries, and convents was that they were being used by the Croatians to store weapons. It was a lie, of course, but a serviceable one. The moment circumstances permitted, they would use it again, to take this convent, and there would be nothing that Father Svet or anyone else could do to stop them.

At the moment, Bosnia-Hercegovina was still a part of the shattered federation known as Yugoslavia. But the yearning for freedom which had infected the two breakaway republics to the north was contagious; sentiment, at least among the Muslims and Croatians which comprised two thirds of the republic's population, was running strongly in favor of following their lead. Anticipating this, the army had long ago stockpiled enough supplies around Mostar to wage a major campaign that would either keep Bosnia-Hercegovina in Yugoslavia, or secure as much of its territory as possible, for Communist Greater Serbia.

Nominally the army was still under civilian control, though in reality it operated autonomously, as it moved to put down "the forces of unrest." It had invited the reservists and civilian irregulars to Mostar, to counter the strength of the Croatians in Hercegovina. The reservists had their own interests at stake. These former professional soldiers, nearly all Serbs, received pensions that enabled them to live better than most civilians in Serbia, and the Senior officers, far better. Since those pensions, like the federal army's payroll, were paid from the government's treasury, and since the army already consumed 70% of

Yugoslavia's gross national product, the departure of Slovenia, Croatia, and now possibly Bosnia-Hercegovina, would put an end to that lifestyle. As for the civilian irregulars, they had left menial jobs in Serbia, for a chance for adventure—and a good deal more.

For nearly three months, the reservists and civilian irregulars had waited for the army to initiate operations in Hercegovina. Now they were growing impatient; perhaps, as in the early days of the war, the irregulars would have to do the initiating themselves.

"They are attempting to provoke an incident," said Father Svet sadly, in another conversation. "But the Croatian people know it, and so they are refusing to let pride get the better of them." What sort of things were they doing? "They go into restaurants and order big meals, lots of wine, then refuse to pay. One reservist left as payment—and a sign—three bullets." What about Medjugorje? "The same as before: tense but calm." There were no soldiers there yet. But each week they moved a little closer.

What about refugees? There were rumors flying around America that the village was inundated with families fleeing the battle zones, and that four thousand refugees were on their way there even now, with thousands more soon to follow.

Father Svet was stunned. "How can people say such things? There are no refugees here. None!" He thought for a moment. "Maybe there are fifty people who lost their homes, living here now with relatives. And all told, maybe four hundred people have stayed with friends or family here, on their way to somewhere else. But that's all! Over in Mostar, there are only six hundred, even now." Where do most of the refugees go, then? "To Split. That's where the Church has its relief center" (and where Father Svet had donated all the proceeds from his most recent book).

How were the visionaries? There were rumors that Vicka had terminal cancer. "She's fine!" he exclaimed, exasperated. Then he said, "You know, you really ought to come over and see for yourself."

Six days later, December 7, Fr. Svet's editor was in the holding pen at JFK that Yugoslav Airlines used as its departure lounge. Because of the sanctions of the European Community and America, JAT was now the only carrier into Yugoslavia. Previously it had run four flights a week, two from New York and two from Chicago. Now, there only two: the New York flights went first to Chicago, before heading for Belgrade.

Among old hands, a trans-Atlantic flight on JAT was considered the first penance of a pilgrimage. That much had not changed. And there actually were three Medjugorje-bound pilgrims on this flight—an Irish grandmother from Boston who had been before, a working mother from New Jersey, and a retired fire-fighter from Staten Island. Thinking that there would be safety in numbers (even small numbers), the editor joined them.

They reached Belgrade at mid-day and killed the afternoon in the cavernous, nearly-deserted terminal waiting for the one daily flight to Sarajevo, the capital of Bosnia-Hercegovina. Except for the absence of travelers, the only difference was an increased military presence. The soldiers were now carrying submachine guns, instead of sidearms, and there was now a $7 war tax levied at each airport, in addition to the $60 "security fee" before departing JFK. The federal government seemed to be desperately short of hard currency. At the bank in the terminal the official rate of exchange was still 22 dinars to the dollar, as it had been in July. But in the coffee shop, a dollar turned out to be worth 50 dinars.

At Sarajevo, the ride that was supposed to be waiting for them, wasn't. But the terminal, though also vacant, seemed noticeably less gloomy, and one could not help wondering if the difference in mood had anything to do with the fact that they were now in a democratic republic. At 10:30 PM, the little group prayed and decided to hire a car and driver to take them to a hotel in Mostar.

Sarajevo being high in the mountains, the main road south was initially coated with ice. As they descended, the ice disappeared, but now they were entering the region where there had been news reports of men, presumably irregulars, casually shooting at passing cars in the night. Why had their driver, a young Muslim with a family of four and a dog named Brik, been willing to take them on such a long and hazardous trip, so late on Sunday night? Their house needed fuel—oil was also sanctioned, and therefore rationed and extremely expensive on the blackmarket—and the dog needed food.

Reaching the outskirts of Mostar around 2:30 AM, they headed for the Hotel Ruja. In the middle of the city, as they stopped at a light, a parked car they had just passed, now flicked on its lights, pulled out, and joined them at the light. In it were two swarthy men in civilian clothes, late-thirties, mustaches, unshaven, unkempt, grinning—

"Do not look at them!" the driver admonished the editor, keeping his own eyes straight ahead, as the light changed. He turned left; so did the other car. He turned left again; the other car did the same. The editor remembered hearing that many of the civilian irregulars were convicted felons who had been released from prison and given guns to join the war in Croatia, that, in fact, their leader in Mostar was wanted in Australia on six counts of murder. The pilgrims had seen this sort of thing before, in movies; now they were in the movie, experiencing the hand of fear, as its icy fingers reached into their entrails and tightened its grip into a fist.

As they came within sight of the Hotel Ruja, they noted two white military jeeps parked in front, with insignia on the doors—a circle of blue stars. "E.C." their driver exclaimed with relief, and then explained that the vehicles belonged to the European Community monitoring team, assigned to Mostar. The editor looked around; the car which had been shadowing them had disappeared.

The Ruja had no oil, and therefore no heat; they were directed to the Dom Pensione. As they pulled up at the front door, the editor commented on the black crater at the curb in front of them. The driver informed him that it had been on the news the night before: a police car had just been blown up there. The pilgrims hurried inside.

In any Croatian town or village, the police were at the top of the potential target list. At the beginning of the war, before the federal army stopped bothering to justify its actions, a typical scenario was for civilian irregulars to slip into a town and open fire on the police, who would naturally defend themselves. Then the army would come in with tanks "to restore order"—and would never leave. The civilians would then move on to the next town and locate the police station. . . .

After September 20, the Serbian Communists no longer bothered with such pretexts. When the army decided which town would be its next objective, it simply warned the Serbians to leave before the shelling started. If any

Croatians happened to see their Serbians neighbors suddenly fleeing their homes with bundles under their arms, they knew what would be coming in the next day or two.

The following morning, Monday, a representative of the pilgrims' travel agency took them over to Medjugorje. On their way, they gingerly picked their way around half-finished road improvements. Pieces of heavy equipment, graders, bulldozers, and the like, had been left standing at the site for months. No one knew when the work would be resumed; the government had no funds for anything but the war now.

There was very little traffic on the roads, and when they passed a gas station, it became apparent why: there was a line of some forty vehicles waiting for the daily allotment of ten liters (about two and a half gallons). This was the only station open between Mostar and Medjugorje, and the wait was often longer than an hour. Some came each day to get more gas for resale on the blackmarket, but buying blackmarket gas was tricky, as people were known to water the gas. It was safer to buy from this station, and if you had a friend who would endure the wait for you, so much the better.

Medjugorje was as empty as it had been in July. It was eerie to see all the new restaurants and cafes and shops with their bright signs and gaily flapping pennants—while nothing but dust swirled down the new sidewalk of the widened main street. In each establishment, one person waited. Perhaps this was the day the pilgrims would return. . . .

In the dusk of late afternoon, the valley was perfectly still. Even time seemed to hold its breath, and one could imagine oneself being held in the hollow of God's hand. . . . It was hard to believe that two hours to the west and six to the northeast, men were killing one another.

And then, the stillness was broken as a distant shot rang out, and a few minutes later, another. They were not intended to kill—merely to alarm and intimidate, like those which disrupted the night, over in Mostar. The inner peace remained, but things were not the same.

That evening, for the rosary before the Mass, the church was more than half full. And these were all local people; there could not have been more than a dozen outsiders. *Zdravo, Marijo.* . . At 5:40, the rosary stopped, and the only sound was the distant chiming of the new electronic carillon. The visionary Marija was in the church—and so was the *Gospa,* the Blessed Mother. Then the rosary continued, and afterwards, as the congregation sang an old favorite, one could feel the same old thrill, and the joy of being back again. Nothing had changed! At least, not in here.

After Mass, there was an Adoration of the Blessed Sacrament, led by Father Slavko. Periodically, he would pray a meditation—in Croatian, of course, but also in Italian and in German. He was leading a retreat that week; probably there were retreatants from those countries. And then he prayed in English, too, and the new arrivals smiled.

After church, it was dark, and the pilgrims felt their way carefully over the path through the fields. The old woman in whose house they were staying was ecstatic to have them; it had been so long since pilgrims had stayed in her little guestrooms. At dinner, there was the wonderful, dense bread of the region, and the muscular Turkish coffee that worked a strange alchemy in one's lower intestinal tract. It was good to be back.

There being no heating fuel, the rooms were dependent upon portable oil heaters, powered by electricity. Under normal conditions they might have been sufficient, but a cold snap had driven the thermometer down to -10 centigrade, and the heaters were not equal to the task. As you got into bed, you could see your breath, and in the middle of the night you debated for an hour whether it was worth the shock of getting out of bed, to don one more sweater.

In the morning the pilgrims agreed it was the coldest night that any of them had ever experienced. But after quantities of hot (American instant!) coffee and tea, they could laugh about it. Shared adversity was a tradition on pilgrimages, medieval or modern; invariably it brought the pilgrims closer—to one another and to God.

3

The Crisis Within

There was another crisis facing Medjugorje—more threatening than the masses of irregulars, looking for an excuse to attack and annihilate. It was an interior crisis, a crisis of the soul.

Millions of souls had been touched by Medjugorje. Perhaps they had been called to conversion there, or had merely heard of what was happening there, and somehow knew it was true. Perhaps they had been touched by other souls who had been touched by that place. . . .

What was the message of Medjugorje? For ten years, the Blessed Mother had been calling all who had the ears to hear, to:

Convert—put God at the center of your life and keep Him there. Let His will take precedence over yours. Live for Him.

Pray—with the heart, keeping in unbroken communion with your Lord. Pray for others, pray for the lost souls, pray for peace. Pray, believing that your prayers can stop wars. Pray for yourself, believing that your Heavenly Father wants what is best for His child.

Fast—deny those appetites of the flesh that keep your spirit from joining His. Let Him direct the fast (you already know in your heart what He would have you abstain from). Let the flesh suffer, for His sake.

Reconcile—with Her Son first. Ask His forgiveness for all the things you have done that have hurt Him. Then accept His forgiveness and the cleansing of His blood. Then, by His grace, forgive those who have hurt you. And by that grace, become reconciled with them, too. And with those whom you have hurt.

Repent—turn and go the other way. If you are truly sorry for what you have done, then you will want to do the opposite. Ask Him to suggest "works meet for repentance" and do these penances with a grateful heart and a cheerful spirit.

For ten years, pilgrims had been coming to Medjugorje and receiving its message. For many, it was the first time in their lives that God had had their undivided attention for a sustained period. No television or radio or newspapers, no telephones or fax machines, no music-players or other entertainment—none of the myriad distractions of the modern world. Only God. And the visionaries and villagers, the priests and sisters.

In that retreat-like atmosphere, gradually, spirits long dormant, awakened. And like doves, stretched their wings and flew. And joined with the Spirit of God. And realized that this was where they had come from and had always longed to return to. And never wanted to leave again.

For many, after a few days in Medjugorje, not only was it easy to put God first; they could not conceive of doing otherwise. He was real, He loved them, and they *knew* it.

For many, it was hard to leave. They would find themselves emotionally torn—which confused them, because they also looked forward to returning to their loved ones. Some thought it was the specialness of the place and its people; here, at "the edge of heaven," they had experienced a joy and completeness they had never imagined could be real.

Those in the company of wise spiritual directors, learned that what they were feeling was their spirit's fear of being separated from God's Spirit. But in leaving Medjugorje, they would not be leaving God—not unless they chose to. Communion with Him was not limited by time or space. They could take Medjugorje with them, in their hearts.

Indeed, that was the farewell message to pilgrims: when you get home, don't rush about, telling people all you saw and found here. Instead, quietly *live* the messages. *Become* the message of Medjugorje. If you do, the ones whom you love and care for, will be drawn to what you have found. They will want what has so dramatically changed your life. They will ask, and then you may tell them of Medjugorje.

Many pilgrims went home, determined to do just that. They prayed and fasted, they forgave and reconciled, they did penance and strived to maintain communion with God. They protected their quiet times and their devotions, their vows and commitments, as a lioness would her cubs. They were back in the world but no longer of it—and they would not slip back.

Many succeeded. And the Lord used the meek, silent witness of their lives to draw others to what had changed them. Medjugorje centers arose, and the flow of pilgrims increased.

But others found that the temptations of the world were more subtle than they had supposed, and discovered that the self-will of their soul was much stronger than they realized. Their determination weakened, and their zeal flagged. No longer did the mention of Medjugorje elicit a smile of joy remembered; instead, there was often the wince of conscience pricked. Or a sigh—as for a lovely but fading dream.

When they were here, they had known that Medjugorje was reality. The cataracts had slipped from their eyes, and they knew they were being given a glimpse of eternal Truth. What the world claimed was reality was but a temporal thing, a drop in the ocean of eternity. But once they re-entered the world they had known, they allowed it to re-enter them. The enemy of the soul began to whisper that what they had experienced over there was not real but a fantasy, a spiritual Shangri-la.

Some returned to Medjugorje, desperate to recapture their perspective, to refresh their spirits and renew their commitment. Sometimes they succeeded; for a few, Medjugorje became almost a commute.

For those pilgrims willing to do battle in their souls to preserve what they had found in Medjugorje, to nurture it and make it grow, gradually a new spirituality took root and deepened in their lives. They embarked on the Way of the Cross, and discovered that while dying out to self was invariably painful, God always provided sufficient grace to anesthetize the pain. Their tap roots went down and anchored them, so that others could hang onto them in storms.

But others on the same path eventually reached a point where they no longer wanted to embrace the cross which God had given them to bear. They had had enough of the pain of dying to self. And the moment they said "Enough," Medjugorje began to fade.

From the beginning, part of the message of Medjugorje

had been to pray for peace. Thousands—then hundreds of thousands—prayed, believing. And the greatest miracle of the twentieth century occurred: Communism collapsed.

Ten years ago, Communism bestrode the globe like a great stone Colossus. It was more than an ideology, more than a social system. It was a corporate spirit, and it was determined to rule the planet. The free world's democracies were powerless to slow its advance, much less contain it. After trying for forty years, the best they could do was assure their mutual destruction. If it came to global war, all civilization would perish.

Then God's messenger called for all who loved her Son, to pray for peace, and a new corporate spirit was born. *Mir,* the Croatian—and Russian—word for peace was written in the sky, and around the world Mir Groups began to form. The prayer continued, with more and more joining in and praying with the heart. And the new spirit, gentle as a breeze, warm as invisible sunlight, wafted around the Colossus.

And then, the impossible happened, the thing which absolutely no one had foreseen. Without any warning, in the twinkling of an eye—peacefully—the Colossus toppled forward on its face, and shattered.

The Sovietologists were dumbfounded. The pundits were speechless. But the Mir Groups only smiled. Had she not said that prayer could stop wars?

But Communism was a system, not a war. It had, to be sure, caused most of the wars in recent memory, but it was not Communism to which she had been referring.

What happened after the fall of Communism has happened so many times in the history of God and man, one would think we might have learned by now. The Bible has laid the pattern: God's people cry out to Him for succor or deliverance. They pray with the heart. He hears their prayer and has mercy on them and pours out His grace. Mightily blessed, they grow complacent. They depart from His way—and so grieve His Spirit that He departs from them. And before long, they find themselves in great need once again.

With Communism no longer a dominant force on the world stage, did we continue to pray for peace with the same fervor as before? Even now that it had become abundantly clear why she had been calling for us to pray for peace for so long, were we?

Many were. But many were not—not if one judged by the mounting urgency of her monthly appeals for prayer. In November, all she could say was: *Pray, pray, pray!*

Were enough of us praying? And were we praying enough? If we were, then the village would be spared. If not. . . .

That was the interior crisis which Medjugorje now faced: her fate rested in our hands.

4

Medjugorje Under Siege

There was no question that the exterior crisis facing the village was coming to a head. Two days before that quiet Friday afternoon on Mt. Krizevac, Father Svet had driven his friend over to Medjugorje. As he guided his faithful white Volkswagen up the hairpin turns out of the valley, he pointed out the reservists' observation posts and fortified positions on the top of practically every hill and mountain since they had left Mostar—all new, since September 20th. They held all the high ground, and in each emplacement someone with binoculars was observing the road.

As they approached the little red-roofed village of Miljkovici, some nine kilometers from their destination, the diminutive Franciscan abruptly pulled to the side of the road and stopped, pointing to a new cement blockhouse on the next hill. The sun was bright that morning, and his friend squinted to see what Father Svet was seeing. There was movement at the blockhouse; a figure emerged from its door, then another, and another.

"Reservists," murmured Father Svet, shaken. "I have never seen them this close to Medjugorje."

His friend wanted to get out and go closer, to get them on video, but the young-old priest shook his head. "They are looking for an incident. Let us not be it. Besides," he smiled grimly, "if you get yourself in prison, maybe not even your embassy could get you out." His friend would have to do the filming through the windshield.

Father Svet started the car and approached slowly, but not so slowly as to draw unwanted attention. As they passed the blockhouse, his friend kept the video camera out of sight. Looking back, he counted nine of them in brown uniforms, deploying down the slope of the little hill, through the leafless winter cover. Their helmets were a strange shape, double-tiered like a stepped bowl. The sun glinted off them, giving them an eerie appearance: they looked like an infestation of shiny brown beetles.

A kilometer or so on the other side of the village, Father Svet and his friend came to a checkpoint manned by two young Croatian policemen in grey uniforms. There was a little corrugated shed to provide some shelter, and two sections of steel I-beams welded together so to form a blockade when moved into position. Father Svet slowed, and the policemen, recognizing him, smiled and waved him through. But Father Svet gave only a half- hearted smile in return. He was still seeing the reservists on the hill.

There were two possible responses to the looming menace which threatened to cast the shadow of its black wings over Medjugorje. On that same Friday, even as the people who had accompanied Mirjana and Father Slavko to the summit of Mt. Krizevac sang *Ave Maria,* down in the valley there was another song being sung, and it was far from soft and gentle.

Across the street from the rectory was the Cafe Dubrovnik, a favorite meeting place in the village. It was a downstairs restaurant, reminiscent of a Bavarian rathskeller, and that afternoon some two dozen men had gathered, prior to going off to join the Croatian National Guard. They were singing old Croatian songs, some dating back more than two centuries—and so fierce was their joy, it put frost on the editor's backbone.

To be there, sipping coffee and listening to them, was like being in a time warp. Half a century had rolled away, and one was in the opening reel of a French film of the thirties, of men going off to war. But the editor had seen this movie before. Too soon, the second reel would play— the mind-numbing, earth-shaking hell of bombardment, the relentless machine-gun fire cutting down all the brave young men. And he would never forget the final reel— the devastated countryside, the broken trees and crumbled buildings, the broken bodies flung casually aside, the mourning women moving among them. . . .

But the men singing in the Dubrovnik could only see the present. Five thousand of their countrymen had lost their lives; five hundred thousand had been driven from their ancestral homes. But as the resistance became organized, it was stiffening—and soon they would be part of it. The time for pay-back was approaching.

As they sang to the memory of an old Croatian hero, Duke Jelacic, calling on him to rise from his grave now that Croatia needed him, the editor shuddered: this was no movie; it was happening.

II

The Past

5

I am the Life

On the low, sandy peninsula with its towering oak trees, the dune grass bent before the southerly wind—as it had for the past three days. A hunting party, clad in buckskin against the onset of winter, watched the ship on the horizon, sailing to and fro, trying to round the elbow of the cape—as it had been for three days. It was rare for the wind to blow from the south this long, and none of them could remember it remaining so strong that one had to lean into it.

They had seen such ships before—two last summer, one the summer before. One had even come close enough for them to see that it was like a huge canoe with great white skins stretched over stripped saplings to catch the wind. There were men on it, with pale flesh and hair on their faces. Recalling that, the youngest of the men now watching wondered if they might be spirits in human form. Their leader scowled at him; spirits would have the power to shift the wind.

Aboard the Mayflower, the Pilgrim elders were in a quandary: their patent specified that their colony was to be in the Virginia Territory, which began at the Hudson River. But the December storm which had driven them across the Atlantic had also blown them considerably north. Their landfall in the New World had been the cape known for the abundance of codfish in its bay; they would have to sail south to clear the cape before heading west for the Hudson.

For the past three days, however, the wind was like a wall before them, and the most fervent prayer could not prevail against it. They had no choice but to conclude that God did not want them in the Virginia Territory. But here was their dilemma: they were to be under the jurisdiction of the Virginia Company, but east of the Hudson, they were under—no one.

They would have to create their own government. And they would have to do so quickly, for there were strangers among them.

They already had a church government which had served them well for the past thirteen years in Holland. Taken from the example of the Early Church, it was made up of elders elected by the congregation—prayerfully elected, for they did their best to hear in their hearts whom God would have lead them. Could they not institute a civil government on the same pattern?

Government by the consent of the governed—democracy, in other words. It had not been tried since ancient Greece; indeed, this was the first instance in modern history of man ever being in a position to create his own government. But it felt right, and in the captain's cabin on that cold, blustery afternoon in November of 1620, they drew up the document that would become known as the Mayflower

Compact. Providing the model for all subsequent civil government in the New England Colonies, it was the cornerstone of American democracy. It began: "In the name of God, amen."

The American people have never known anything but democracy. With the exception of a few brief years under the British king, George III, they have never lived under tyranny.

With the exception of a few brief years many centuries ago—and the past two years—the Croatian people have never known anything else. At the time the Mayflower reached Cape Cod, the Croatians had already suffered nearly three centuries of ruthless domination by the Ottoman Turks. Our intellects can understand their past— but our collective hearts have no memory to compare to it. We cannot know the desperation with which they have yearned to be free.

If God governs in the affairs of men, then the contrasts in our histories bear noting. For while in the beginning the Americans may have been given grace beyond reckoning, in the end it was the Croatians who, through the furnace of their unending affliction, were better prepared for the unimaginable blessing awaiting them.

The arrival of the Pilgrims proved to be the defining moment of our civilization. In their humble life together, with the Lord at their center, they exemplified our spiritual heritage. Jesus had said: *I am the Way, the Truth, and the Life.* . . Others in the seventeenth century were preaching that He was the Way, others were teaching that He was the Truth. It fell to the Pilgrims to show that He was the life.

They came in meekness, and in peace. And the world was a better place, for their having lived in it. In their gentle caring for one another, and for all who came in contact with them, Jesus could be seen. Through them, others were drawn to Him. And these others, too, began to live the Life. Other groups would come later, just as devoted, just as given. But the Pilgrims were the first.

We have fallen far short of their example, but we have never forgotten it. And sometimes, when a church or a prayer group or a campus—or a group of modern pilgrims—comes to life in their spirit, we rediscover what they knew. But we will never know how much the grace that is still on this land is the fruit of the givenness of our forebears.

By the grace of God, our three and a half centuries have been shaped by the ones who were given being in the right place at the right time. Before the Pilgrims, there were missionaries—in robes of black or brown or grey, they dwelt among the Indians, learning their language, eating their food. . . . They lived the Life—and through their example the Indians were drawn to the Life-giver, who freed them from the fear they had always known. ("Evangelize, evangelize!" St. Francis had once exhorted his followers. "And if you must, use words.")

After the Pilgrims came the Puritans and the Huguenots and the Moravians—and the Catholics who named their colony after their beloved Mary. After them, there were God's lightning rods on horseback, riding up and down the eastern seaboard to awaken the Colonies spiritually—and prepare them (though none knew it) for the trial to come. When the world expected the fledgling nation to be quickly crushed, the faith of the given stood in the gap for those who could not believe.

When it came time to frame the new republic's constitution, men of faith employed wisdom beyond their ken. Then Methodist circuit-riders transformed the frontier, and Quakers were the first to come against the spirit of slavery. Other pioneers whose names will never be known, lived the Life and bore its light across the Continent. In the war in which brother killed brother, the prayers of countless thousands more in blue uniforms and gray, were instrumental in moderating that horrible ordeal, and healing this land.

By the grace of God, more than a century has passed since the last shot was fired within our borders by one soldier intending to kill another, and a half-century more, since the last foreign invader was driven from our land. Since then, we have been to war many times, but war has never come to us—not to this soil, not with shells raining down on our homes, and our family or friends being killed in the next town or the next street. We can read about such agony, hear about it and watch it on the news. We can be struck with horror, filled with compassion. But we cannot *know* it.

By the grace of God, we are a people who have never known anything but freedom—the freedom to speak our minds and worship as we please. The freedom to set goals and attain them, if we have the will for it and the discipline. The freedom to refuse to do what we don't feel like doing. As a people, with the exception of the blacks, we have never known how it feels to be forced to do what we don't want to do, to be denied all right of redress, to be persecuted for simply being who we are. We have never known how it feels to live under the constant threat of annihilation. To wake up and wonder if this will be our last day on earth.

And now by the grace of God, with the exception of those who served in Viet Nam, a whole generation of Americans has known nothing but peace.

In the fourteen centuries since the first Serbs and Croatians migrated into the region known as Hercegovina, there has never been a generation which has known peace. Every newcomer to their land was an invader. The insignia on the banners leading their columns might change, but the methods of subjugation and administering fear would be all too familiar. This has been their lot—which began a thousand years before the Pilgrims brought the Life to the New World.

Our history is as incomprehensible to them, as theirs is to us. And then, a little over ten years ago, an extraordinary thing happened: through a continuing miracle of God, they began to know what the Pilgrims knew, the meaning of Jesus' words: *I am the Life*. One village began to live the Life, then more and more. And that village became in spirit what it already was physically, and what Matthew had foretold: a city set upon a hill, that could not be hidden and would give light to the world.

6

East and West

The great strength of the Roman Empire was ascribed to two key attributes: organizational ability and the Rule of Law.

And there was no question that its phenomenal expansion owed much to the efficiency of its central government. But by the end of the second century after the Birth of Christ, it had grown so vast that centralized government had become an administrative and logistical nightmare. It was said that all roads led to Rome—and all of them were clogged with messengers going to and from the capital.

The Emperor Diocletian, surveying a map of the known world which showed his empire encompassing all countries around the Mediterranean (which Romans referred to as *Mare Nostrum,* "Our Sea"), extending northwest to include Britannicum, east to Armenia and Mesopotamia, and southeast to Aegyptus, cried, "Enough!" Subdividing many of the provinces, he separated civil administration from military command—and in 305 A.D. did the ultimate: he divided the entire empire in half.

In the Balkan Peninsula, the line dividing East from West followed the Danube River and then jumped over to the Drina. Included in the Western Roman Empire was nearly all of today's republic of Slovenia, the western half of Croatia, and all of Bosnia-Hercegovina. Serbia, Macedonia, and the eastern half of Montenegro would henceforth be governed from the capital of the Eastern Roman Empire, Byzantium.

After Diocletian, rule over the two empires was simultaneously shared by as many as six *Augusti,* until it was consolidated by the Emperor Constantine. A major step in that consolidation was his victory over Maxentius in 312, for which Constantine gave the credit to God. From that time forward, his letters and edicts indicated that he regarded himself as the servant of the "Highest Divinity," the God of the Christians. He became a Christian himself and proclaimed full toleration of the Christian Church, defeating the last of the Christian persecutors, Lucinius, in 324.

To celebrate the victory, "by the command of God" he founded a new imperial city, rebuilding Byzantium on a magnificent scale. It took six years, but when Constantinople (renamed for its founder) was dedicated in 330, it was a fitting capital of the Roman Empire, both spiritual and secular—indeed, it soon became known as "New Rome."

Old Rome, needless to say, was not pleased. This rival for her splendor was growing yearly more powerful—while her beleaguered mother was now being consumed from within by corruption, and from without by the ever-deeper incursions of the Visigoths, Huns, Vandals, and other barbarian tribes to the north. By 395, the division between the two empires was complete. While the head of the Western Church in Rome was still paid nominal obeisance by the head of the Eastern Church in Constantinople, there was no question that in terms of power, the daughter had supplanted the mother.

There had been differences between the Western and Eastern Churches long before Diocletian and Constantine. In the beginning both Churches worshipped in Greek, but after two centuries the Church in Rome had become Latinized, while the Eastern Church continued to worship in Greek. There were other such cultural differences, but in the early years they were not divisive. The Churches belonged to Jesus Christ, and in Him there was no east or west. Regardless of what language they spoke, or how powerful or weak they were, at the foot of the Cross, they were one.

As long as they were to keep that perspective, there was harmony—or at least, the chance for the restoration of same. But Christians are human, and humans are temptable. And the enemy was listening, when Jesus said: *A house divided against itself shall not stand.* The enemy knew that the one way to neutralize the Body of Christ, was to divide it against itself. And the sin best suited to that purpose was the one which had cost him his place in heaven: pride.

So, in each of the early churches, he sowed his seeds. One church was tempted to believe that it was purer than its sister church to the west (or east or north or south). It was tempted to believe that while the other church might have more wealth or influence or numbers, *its* doctrine was the more correct, and therefore it stood closer to God.

(Jealousy was often the handmaiden of pride.)

Not even the Apostles were immune to such temptation. But by their example, they showed how the spirit of Christianity could—and must—triumph over its form. When Paul heard that Peter was incorporating old Jewish customs into new Christian worship—and teaching that unless a new Christian conformed to these customs, he was not keeping the faith—he confronted Peter. New wine belonged in new wineskins. And Peter, perhaps remembering how God had shown him in a dream that all meat was edible, took Paul's correction to heart and changed.

It took courage for Paul to confront the one of whom the Master had said, *Upon this rock I will build my church.* It may have taken even more courage for Peter to humble himself and admit that he was wrong. Together they offered the model for how the Body of Christ was to heal division.

Some churches followed their example, plucking out the weeds as soon as they sprouted in their garden, and taking care to get all of the root beneath the surface. But other churches enjoyed the aroma and the flavor of the weed, and even developed a taste for it. . . .

Long before Diocletian divided the Roman Empire, such seeds had already been sown in the heart of the underground Christian Church. The formal division only reinforced the differences, and as Rome grew weaker and Constantinople stronger, they came to be regarded as significant.

The Roman Church continued to worship in Latin. (By 450, only a handful of Western scholars could even read Greek). The Eastern Church worshipped in Greek, as it always had. (By 600, only a few Eastern scholars could read Latin.) But as Greek was older than Latin, it was presumably closer to what the first Christians spoke. The New

Testament, after all, was first written in Greek. The Eastern Church came to believe that theirs was the purer form of worship, and they took on the name Orthodox (Greek, for "right belief").

Other differences crystallized: Roman Catholics believed that, as Christ had turned the keys of the Church over to Peter, there could be only one head of the Church, and he was in Rome, as he always had been. The Pope was the ultimate and absolute authority; beneath him— and subservient to him—in a divinely-ordained ecclesiastical nobility were Cardinals and Bishops (or Patriarchs and Metropolitans). The Orthodox, however, believed in a collegiality of leadership, as had existed among the Apostles. The Patriarchs of each Eastern Orthodox nation considered themselves to be brothers in the apostolate— with the Pope merely first among equals.

The West believed in the functional segregation of Church and State; since the aims of the two were often opposed, the Church regarded the State with suspicion, jealous to protect what belonged to God alone. The Eastern Church, considered the State to be the secular arm of God; even an evil State had God's authority. Thus, with rare exception, the Eastern Church was able to work in harmony with the State.

Add to such differences, the natural divergence of cultures (the West put more emphasis on Canon Law, The East on worship and liturgy), politics, and economies, and one could see how easily the two might drift farther and farther apart.

But the greatest cause of division was not in their doctrine or culture, nor in the political and economic vicissitudes of the world at that time; throughout history Christians have overcome such obstacles in their desire to remain united in spirit. *That* was the problem: neither side had such a desire. At best, they were indifferent to one another. When Rome was beset with invading hordes, Constantinople turned her back; the old wanton had it coming. Two centuries later, when Constantinople was buckling under the onslaught of Islam, Rome smiled; finally the young upstart was getting her just desserts.

The only place where they were in perfect agreement was in their refusal to listen to one another. Attempts at reconciliation were made—but neither party could be accused of coming with a meek and open heart. Papal delegates were sent from Rome, not to seek, but to demand. And pride was met with pride; the more right one side got, the more certain the other side became that *they* were right. (It is not so hard to understand—one has only to recall the last time one was confronted, when one was certain that one was being misunderstood.) In the case of Rome and Constantinople, however, the fate of all Christendom hung in the balance.

One cannot help wondering what might have happened, had the delegates on one side or the other prayed for humility—and been willing to be humiliated. Some undoubtedly did, during the numerous attempts to close the widening schism. But each time, sooner or later, spiritual pride re-hardened hearts that had begun to soften. One side would deliberately insult the other, and the other would retaliate in kind, and each would withdraw—to add new points to the growing list of differences which were doctrinally unacceptable.

As is sadly so often the case in such quarrels, the extent of a rift can be gauged by the pettiness of the point in question. (Divorce lawyers refer to this as "the jelly glass syndrome.") In the Nicene Creed of 325, both Churches had agreed that the Holy Spirit proceeded from the Father. But the Western Church began stating that He also proceeded from the Son, and by the time of Charlemagne, Emperor of the Holy Roman Empire at the beginning of the ninth century, the Pope formally approved this addition. This was done without benefit of an Ecumencial Council—which amounted to a political, as well as theological affront.

Other points of contention: the East accepted lay theologians; the West believed that only the clergy should be educated. The East permitted its lower clergy to marry; the West insisted that all its priests remain celibate. During worship, the East remained standing; the West spent more time sitting or kneeling.

By the time the Pope in Rome and the Patriarch in Constantinople excommunicated each other in 1054, each Church was convinced that the other was corrupt beyond redemption.

Each Church forbade its followers to have anything to do with the other, and since in that era it was the greatest single influence on life, how the Church went, the people went. The division grew wider. But until 1204, the hurts on either side were mainly that: hurts to pride. With effort, with prayer, and with softened hearts, they might have been forgiven. And then came the Fourth Crusade.

When the Crusader army assembled at Venice in 1202 for embarkation, they lacked the funds to pay it. The Venetians made them a deal: if the Crusaders would join them in forcing Constantinople to put the pretender Alexius on the Byzantine imperial throne, Alexius would pay their debts. The Crusaders did, but a palace revolution defied them and overthrew Alexius in 1204. Enraged, the Crusaders assaulted the city and sacked it, raping, pillaging, murdering—and earning forever the enmity of Byzantine

Christendom. This was the unforgiveable sin (and eight centuries later, it is still recalled with bitterness).

How deep did such feelings run? Two and a half centuries later, when Consantinople was about to be overwhelmed by the Ottoman Empire, the cry of its inhabitants was: "Better the Turkish turban than the Latin mitre!"

With the fall of Constantinople, and the Orthodox Church in peril, its seat moved further east—to Russia. Moscow became the Third Rome, and Russia was now looked to as the big brother and protector of all the Orthodox nations.

In time, even the Crusaders' sack of Constantinople might have been forgiven. . . . But the enemy taught people how to hate—for hatred was the wedge which kept the walls of a split from closing. And once a people had begun to hate, he knew exactly how to drive the wedge deeper.

7

Serb and Croatian

When the Slavic peoples known as the Serbs and the Croatians began migrating over the Carpathian Mountains and down into the Balkan Peninsula in the seventh century, they found the land sparsely occupied by the Illyrians. According to Greek mythology, these descendents of Illyricus, the son of the Cyclops Polyphemus and the sea nymph Galatea, left Sicily to settle on the eastern shores of the Adriatic. According to modern archaeologists, they had been there since man began to make tools from iron, instead of bronze, about a millennium before the birth of Christ.

As the Roman Empire extended its reach inland from the Dalmatian Coast, it named the new province Illyricum, and as it was on an important trade route between Rome and eastern Europe, its people prospered. When the empire receded, and they were repeatedly overrun and devastated by Visigoth and Hun raiding parties, they nonetheless managed to remain more or less intact. But the Serbs and

Croatians were another matter; they were coming to live. By the seventh century, the Illyrians in Dalmatia, Croatia, Bosnia, Serbia, Montenegro, and parts of Macedonia had been completely slavonized. Only the Albanians would remain as their direct descendents.

In the ninth century, two brothers from Thessalonika, Cyril and Methodius, undertook to complete the Christianization of all the Slavs. First, they invented a Slavic alphabet based on Greek letters, which in its final form would be called Cyrillic (and is still used by all Slavs of the Eastern Church). Then using it, they translated the Bible into what would become known as Old Church Slavonic. Canonized by both the Eastern and Western Churches, more than anyone else Cyril and Methodius were responsible for the spread of Christianity among Serbs and Croatians.

These two peoples, who spoke the same language, worshipped the same God, arrived at the same time, and settled in lands adjacent to one another, would appear to have had much in common. But East was East, and West was West; the dividing line went down between them, and a thousand years ago the two Churches pretty much decided how their people would feel about each another. The Serbs took their lead from Constantinople; the Croatians from Rome.

As it happened, the parish of Konjic, on a southeastern bend of the Neretva River was—and is—the easternmost Franciscan parish in Hercegovina. There is a monastery there, and until recently Father Svet was one of its friars. He helped build, and then served as pastor of a small church high on the side of one of Konjic's mountains. From the steps of his church late one July afternoon last summer, he pointed out different rooftops below. This one belonged to a Serbian family, next to them lived a Muslim family, next to them a Croatian family. The sun was setting, and the village was quiet; it was almost supper-time. Only the children were out, playing together in front of their houses.

"It is peaceful here," murmured Father Svet to a friend. "It has been, for a long time." He paused. "These people have no hard feelings towards one another. They have different religions, but they get along well." It was true; not only did they allow their children to play together, but earlier that afternoon each family had smiled and waved to him as he passed.

In the Balkans, as elsewhere, the history of the eleventh, twelfth and thirteenth centuries was an endless series of minor conflicts, as first one group then another attempted to either wrest land from their neighbors or gain power over them—just as their ancestral tribes had, since the dawn of civilization. Only in the Balkans, these struggles seemed more intense. Perhaps it was the harshness of the mountainous terrain, or the difficulty with which men wrung a living from the soil, or the readiness of the Slavic temperament to put action behind words, and once-committed, to fight to the death. Whatever the reason, there was no respite in their strife, no brief footnote of a generation which had known peace.

Each land—Serbia, Croatia, Bosnia—had its time in the sun, its one shining chapter. Their monarchs would triumph, their armies would extend their borders at the expense of their neighbors. And then the wave which had stretched so far would recede, and another wave would come. . . But their identity as a people was established;

regardless of what the latest maps might indicate, they would always be a nation—even if only in their hearts. And once a people had known ascendancy, that shining chapter was there forever in their memory, to tantalize and goad. They were a nation, and a nation needed a homeland.

For the Croatians, the influence of Rome was brought closer to home in the fourteenth century, with the arrival of the Franciscans. To the Order of St. Francis, the Pope had entrusted the watchcare of his easternmost subjects, and these brown-robed friars, vowed to poverty and selfless service, came to live among the Croatians, sharing their hardships and becoming part of their life. Monasteries were established, a seminary was founded, and the faith grew deeper.

In Bosnia, with Serbia to the east and Croatia to the north and west, the faith encountered a major obstacle— a powerful sect known as the Bogomils. The king of Bosnia was a Bogomil, as were all the nobles. The Bogomils, believing that the visible, material world was created by the devil, lived in extreme asceticism. They had no use for Christian baptism or the Eucharist or miracles or the Cross—or, for that matter, the entire organization of the Orthodox Church.

Then the leader of the Franciscan order met with the Bosnian king, and in this case, the immovable object gave way to the irresistible force. In 1339, the king became a Christian, and within four years there were 36 monasteries in his realm. The rest of his nobles, however, did not follow his lead, and the rivalry between the two religions grew heated. All the while, Hungarians and Croatians continued to struggle to see who would rule the land, and Bosnia acquired the province which would one day be known as Hercegovina ("dukedom"). By the middle of the fourteenth century, Hungarians, Croatians, Serbs, and Bogomils all had something more ominous to consider: the Turks were coming.

Having repelled the Crusaders, Islam was on the march. The Turks found that in addition to an aptitude for organization and a singleness of purpose, they had a taste for *jihad* (holy war). The Ottoman Empire conquered in all directions, and in 1386 it invaded Bosnia, extending as far south and west as the Neretva River. The Serbs fared less well, being disastrously defeated at Kosovo in 1389. Turkish rule extended the length of Serbia, most of Croatia, and the northern half of Bosnia—all of which would remain part of the Ottoman Empire for the next four centuries.

The Turks, now in control of Constantinople, made a generous peace with Serbia, allowing it to retain much of its freedom in exchange for becoming a vassal state. And to the Bogomil nobles in Bosnia, they made an offer they could not refuse: if they would convert to Islam, the nobles could keep all their properties. Most did convert (many of the Muslims in Bosnia-Hercegovina today are their descendents). But those Croatians who did not flee north, were another story. For they remained faithful to the Church in Rome, and Rome continued to be the most obstinate adversary the Ottoman Empire faced.

In Bosnia, to weaken the hold of Rome and destabilize the region which had been under control of the Catholic Church for eight centuries, the Turks brought in Orthodox Serbs and settled them there. As anticipated, the two faiths started contending—and made it far easier for the Turks to rule.

It was a dark time for the Croatians under Turkish dominion. As in all totalitarian regimes, the Turks maintained control through administering fear. And as always, a non-cooperative Church became the greatest potential danger. For as long as people believed, they could not be intimidated. They might be made afraid, but they did not allow fear to dictate their decisions. So the Church had to be eradicated. Worship was forbidden; priests were hunted down as outlaws and killed.

But the priests did not leave. The spiritual life of the people had been entrusted into their care; they would not abandon their charges. They hid in the mountains, crept down at night under cover of darkness, to serve Communion, perform weddings, baptize children, administer the last rites to the dead. Whenever they were caught, they were slaughtered. But they did not leave. And the people never forgot.

When Father Svet was a child, each year his mother would take him to the site of such a massacre. The Turks had come upon a group of people in the hills worshipping with their priest, and they had killed them all. More than four centuries had passed since they were martyred, yet to his mother it was still fresh. As her little boy sat on a rock and watched, she knelt and on her knees made her way around the perimeter, praying as she went. It was a sight that would stay with him the rest of his life.

Nor was her faith unusual; that was what happened to people who had lived for so long under the possibility of instant death, if they were caught in the act of worship. They never stopped—and the tap-root of their faith went so deep that the darkest tornado could not uproot it.

In the middle of the nineteenth century, the Austrians and the Hungarians and the rest of Western Europe prevailed over the Ottoman Empire. The Balkans were liberated—but not freed. Serbs and Croatians were still under foreign domination—Catholic, perhaps, and more tolerant, but foreign. The Orthodox Serbs still looked to Russia as their protector, but Russia was absorbed with her own problems.

Meanwhile, the Austrians were aware of how much the Croatians yearned for independence and a homeland— so much that they might even reach a rapport with the neighboring Serbs—and that could prove difficult. To forestall such an eventuality and ensure that peace between the two would never break out, the Austrians installed Serbian paramilitary groups in the region of Croatia known as Krajina.

And so the Balkans continued to be a seething cauldron of frustrated nationalism. Finally as the twentieth century dawned, the South Slavs were willing to explore various amalgamations, if that was the only way to achieve a measure of autonomy. With Serbia's defeat of the Turks in the Balkan Wars of 1912-13, that now became a possibility. But then, a year later, a Serb nationalist assassinated Austria's Archduke Ferdinand, as he visited the capital of Sarajevo. Austria-Hungary declared war on Serbia, and soon the entire world was drawn into what became known as the Great War.

8

Chetniks and Ustase

Sometimes patience, of all the virtues, is the most difficult to retain—especially for a people who by temperament are given to action. For more than a thousand years, Serbs and Croatians had dreamed of the day when they would have their own homeland, free and clear of foreign domination. And each, having once savored autonomy, would never forget its taste. The Croatians desired the restoration of their pre-Turkish borders, as did most Serbs. But there were elements in Belgrade which desired something more.

Nations are like people, with personal responses to different situations. They are like people, because they *are* people—the sum of their populace. A nation, then, becomes a corporate projection of its individual citizens' sins and virtues. Unredeemed man is by nature selfish and acquisitive, and the people of Europe are no different than people anywhere else. From the beginning of their recorded history, one European tribe had striven with another for land or wealth or domination. Sometimes the tribes would band together into a kingdom, and sometimes that kingdom would expand into an empire; in the long view, they were like bubbles forming and subsiding in the magma of an active volcano.

Christianity was the force which could change all that. Under its inspiration, a man, or a nation, could desire—and choose—to stand against its natural aggression. It could choose peace, instead of war; meekness, instead of pride. It was not the natural choice; it was supernatural. But it could happen, and it had: nations where Christian faith was strong, preferred peace. They would still go to war, but only with reluctance, and only when it had become a moral imperative, to defend their homeland or to put a stop to evil aggression.

Yet even these could be seduced by pride or the lust for power. There were in Serbia certain men who reflected the mindset which had prevailed in Europe for centuries. Their dream extended beyond their existing borders, to include their neighbors—and all of the Balkan peninsula. They dreamed of Greater Serbia.

This dream which had long existed as a myth, was first spelled out in 1844, by the Internal Affairs Minister of the Principality of Serbia: Serbia could not be allowed to remain a small country but must increase its territory without fail, and that expansion was to be achieved beyond its historic and ethnic borders. At the beginning of the twentieth century, Serbian anthropo-geographic research "proved" that of all the people in the Balkans, the Serbs were the most "valuable." Therefore, they had the right to include in their state all regions in which Serbs lived.* "Where

---

*Croatia Between War and Independence, University of Zagreb, 1991.

one Serb lives, there is Serbia." With the October Revolution of 1917 in Russia, their great protector, they wondered if the new Communism might not help them achieve the dream.

Following the defeat of Austria-Hungary at the end of the Great War, the South Slavs suddenly had what they had almost given up hoping for: freedom to chart their own destiny. Most felt that the only way to preserve that freedom was to join together in a new democracy, and they did: the State of the Slovenes, Croats and Serbs was inaugurated of October 29, 1918, with its duly-elected government, the National Council, located in Zagreb.

It lasted thirty-five days. In Belgrade, Alexander, the regent of Serbia, had a different view of their collective future: a Kingdom of Serbs, Croats and Slovenes—with himself as the king. Through duplicity and adroit (albeit illegal) maneuvering, the sovereignty of the new state was abolished on December 3, the National Council in Zagreb being replaced by the National Assembly in Belgrade.

At first, the Croatians had hopes of equality under the new regime. But the deputies to the National Assembly were appointed rather than elected, and within a year Alexander had dissolved the Croatian Parliament which had been in existence for a thousand years. In November, 1920, a Constitutional Assembly was convened for the purpose of deciding whether the state would continue as a republic or a monarchy. But before the delegates were admitted to the convention, they were required to take an oath of loyalty to the king. Deputies from Croatia and Slovenia left the assembly before the vote, so that there would not be a quorum, but the vote was taken anyway, and the Kingdom of Serbs, Croats and Slovenes came into being.

Eight years later, Stjepan Radic, the charismatic, non-violent leader of the Croatian Peasants' Party, and two deputies were shot to death in the National Assembly. Alexander, under the influence of his Prime Minister, General Zhivkovic and other ultra-nationalists, declared a royal dictatorship and renamed his country Yugoslavia ("Kingdom of the South Slavs"). He instituted a common currency, the Serbian dinar, which replaced the *kruna* which had been in use in Croatia, Slovenia, and Bosnia-Hercegovina. Though the two had been roughly equal in value, the exchange rate was set at four krunas to the dinar.

His biggest problem, Alexander saw, would be the subjugation of the Croatian people, and the burden for accomplishing it fell on the state's security police. What they could not do, was done by their auxiliary, militant groups of ultra-nationalists known as *Chetniki* ("freedom fighters") who commenced terrorizing Croatians everywhere.*

Without the filter of a cleansing and renewing faith, patriotism can very quickly cease to be a virtue and metamorphose into something darker. The line between ultra-nationalism and fascism is often so fine that what you call it depends on whether it is wearing your uniform or theirs.

In any society, two things guarantee civilized behavior: accountability to God, and respect for the law. Wherever there is not a strong faith, there had better be a strong— and universally trusted—police force. For when there is no accountability, man is capable of dark deeds—that grow progressively darker, the longer they are condoned.

---

*Trying to tell the story of Chetnik and Ustase is like trying to tell about the Civil War—in 1910—from Charleston—with North and South suddenly re-joined in mortal combat.

As the police looked the other way, the Chetniks committed atrocities so horrendous—killing children in front of their parents and vice versa, burying people alive in graves they had been forced to dig, mutilating the bodies of the slain—that the word Chetnik became synonymous with the most bestial behavior of one man towards another. (This had happened before—in the Soviet Union, the secret police kept having to change its name and initials, from the Cheka to the NKVD to the MVD to the KGB—because of the dread and loathing of the people whom they were protecting.)

This was more than the madness which sometimes gripped men who, having conquered a city, and intoxicated with limitless power and no accountability, did things they would spend the rest of their lives trying to forget. This Chetnik darkness continued for years. It was what happened when the enemy took over men who had long held the doors of their hearts open to him. They ceased to behave like human beings and became like beasts—the hideous creatures described by those permitted to see visions of hell.

Hell is where they came from, and unmuzzled, hell is what they unleashed on earth. Nor did they stop at killing; they fell on the lifeless bodies of their prey, rending and mutilating in a frenzy of hatred. They scorned love, mocking it at every opportunity, reveling in their victory over it, and crucifying it again, if they could. They were the body of Satan on earth.

The Croatian people were doubly outraged, because they were powerless to respond, and because they were a proud people who had been made afraid. They would never forget.

And in time, they had their own ultra-nationalist faction: the *Ustase*, which meant "Stand up." In the beginning, the great majority of Croatians were sympathetic to them, if not actively involved. Finally, someone was standing up to the Chetniks and putting a stop to their wanton depredations.

Passionately committed to achieving a Croatian homeland, the Ustase was determined to do so—by whatever means it took. (And perhaps that is where Christianity applies its ultimate filter: no matter how noble or desirable the end, it never justifies immoral means.) And because they reflected the desire that was in every Croatian's heart, many moral men chose to ignore their excesses.

The priests counseled patience. But it seemed to some men, that sometimes their beloved Franciscans were more in touch with heaven than with earth. The time for patience was past. It was time for Croatia to throw off the yoke of the bloody tyrant and have a homeland of her own!

Ultra-nationalists have a taste for revenge. It is, as the saying goes, a dish best savored cold—and hate, properly bottled and stored, keeps surprisingly well. All it takes is for parents to be certain that their children know exactly what has been done to their grandparents and by whom. Once the bottles have been filled, corked, and sealed, they can be taken down to the cool, dark cellar and placed in racks. All that is required is make sure the corks do not dry and admit air which turns the wine to vinegar. And one must occasionally rotate the bottles—it never hurts to remind the children every so often. . . .

King Alexander was assassinated by Ustase agents in 1934. Once again there was a brief movement towards equality, and once again it was stifled by extremists. The Ustase leadership, now in exile in Italy under the protection of Mussolini, still dreamed of an independent Croatian state, possibly brought into being by the Fascists. As the years passed, the dream came closer. In 1939, Mussolini invaded Albania; in 1940, Greece.

But by now the Ustase had seen that it was Hitler, not Mussolini who could guarantee their dream. The Führer got the job done—and he was a mesmerizer. Many who would never dream of shooting out their arms to salute him before, now intoxicated with his conquests, shouted *"Sieg heil!"* with the rest.

In the spring of 1941, with Europe beneath his feet, and the British lion gasping, Hitler now turned his concentration eastward. But first he needed to secure his right flank. In a secret pact, he persuaded the Yugoslav government to throw in with the Axis Powers, guaranteeing that they would be treated as neutrals. But when the people of Yugoslavia found out, they overthrew their government.

Hitler flew into a rage—the first of his great rages, and by eyewitness accounts, more towering than any which followed. Apoplectic with fury, he made his greatest error of judgment—the one which, his generals later agreed, cost him the war. Operation Barbarossa, the invasion of Russia, was scheduled for the beginning of May, 1941. Now it was delayed, while Hitler wrought vengeance on Yugoslavia for betraying him. Army Group South was diverted down into Yugoslavia, and Austria, Hungary, Italy, and Bulgaria were invited to participate.

On April 10th they all attacked—from every direction. Its army overwhelmed, Yugoslavia fell in ten days. But with all the distraction and redirection of logistics, and all the re-coordinating that needed to be done, Barbarossa was delayed five weeks. And Russia's greatest ally, winter, which had defeated Napoleon and all other invaders from the west, now stopped the Nazis at the gates of Moscow—one month short of their goal.

All of the peoples of Yugoslavia were now under the subjugation of their Nazi and Fascist conquerors. All save one—the Croatians. Hitler created the *Nezavisna Drzava Hrvatska* or NDH (Independent State of Croatia), and put the Ustase in charge. Initially, for many Croatians it seemed a dream come true—and they chose not to consider that they had made a pact with evil incarnate.

But the face of evil was revealed soon enough. The Ustase had some long scores to settle, and under the NDH they now took revenge on all the Chetniks they could find. Eventually, their decanted hatred spilled over on all Serbs, regardless of whether they had ever had anything to do with the Chetniks. It was pay-back time.

According to published accounts, Mile Budak, the NDH minister of education, had been in office less than two months when he announced the Ustase's solution to the problem of what to do with the Serbs: some would be deported, some would be killed, and some would be converted to Catholicism and turned into Croatians.

But history is written by the victors. . . . What cannot be disputed is that a Nazi-style concentration camp was erected at Jasenovic, to which were shipped thousands of Serbs, Jews, and Gypsies—as well as increasing numbers of Croatians who, faced with mounting evidence of Ustase atrocities, could no longer remain silent.

The Ustase claimed that they were only doing to the Serbs what the Chetniks had done to the Croatians—as if such unspeakable barbarism somehow justified its perpetuation. This, then, was what the radicalized Ustase had become—the beast that good people unmuzzled, when they could not be patient a little longer. And now good people felt compelled to speak out against their crimes, though it might cost them their lives.

Meanwhile, powerless and afraid, all Serbs within the reach of the Ustase fled to the mountains or to the resistance—and sent newly-filled bottles down to the cellar. They would not have long to wait; the tide of battle was turning.

9

The Rise and Fall of Communist Yugoslavia

When the Russians held at Stalingrad in the winter of 1942, the outcome of the war in Europe was sealed. Short on supplies and shorter on fuel, the Germans struggled to keep their retreat along the Eastern Front from turning into a rout. Never again would they regain the initiative. The following year, their vaunted spring offensive was two months late—and lasted a week. The Thousand-Year Reich was about to end 990 years ahead of schedule.

In Yugoslavia, the leaders of the resistance could see the writing on the wall. By the end of 1943, some 300,000 people were actively involved in the resistance, 26 divisions in all. Of them, eleven were Croatian, seven Bosnia-Hercegovinian, five Slovenian, two Serbian, and one Montenegrin. The resistance was far from united: there were Croatian antifacists, Serbian antifascists, and Communist *Partizani* under Josip Broz, who called himself Tito. More concerned about who was going to rule after the Germans left, the three factions began fighting each other, rather than their common enemy.

Which left the Allies in a quandary: which of these three should they back, or should they try to be even-handed? In the end, winning the war as quickly as possible could be their only consideration, and a unified resistance in Yugoslavia would best accomplish this. Of the three factions, only Tito's Partisans seemed to be primarily interested in driving the Germans out, so the Allies gave their support to him, knowing that it would almost certainly mean a post-war Communist government in Yugoslavia.

Many Chetniks now cast off their fascist trappings and aligned themselves with the Partisans, embracing the Communist ideology. It did not matter to them whether it was a grey wolf or a red wolf, as long as it was their wolf.

And once the German had departed, they helped the Communists hunt down the Ustase. It was pay-back time.

Thousands upon thousands of Croatians fled north, ahead of the advancing Communists and Chetniks. They were civilians mostly, but among them were antifascist fighters, *domobrans* (Croatian civilians forcibly recruited into the NDH army), and Ustase. Rather than surrender to the Communists and face death or long internment, they were heading for Austria, to surrender to the Allies.

But when they reached the border at Bleiburg, despite the fact that Prime Minister Winston Churchill had said that they could stay in Austria, the local British commander refused to accept them. Instead, he sent them on trains (telling them they were going to Italy) back to the Communists—who had already bulldozed mass graves in preparation for them. In a single day, May 15, 1945, some 16,000 were executed and thrown into these pits. Thousands more perished, as they were driven on brutal death marches to concentration camps.

How many Serbs died in Jasenovic and other camps, how many Croatians died at the hands of the Chetniks and Communists, which extremists committed the more heinous atrocities—depends on whether one is talking to a Serb or a Croat. Tragically each gets so caught up in accusing the other of escalating or suppressing the figure that they totally miss the point: blasphemy was done in the name of patriotism. And it was done over and over and over, by both sides.

There are enough bottles stored in the cellars of both families to keep their descendants drunk for centuries. And the master of those cellars doesn't care who drinks it, as long as they keep sending down for more. It is a vintage wine, this hatred between Serb and Croat; it has produced a generation of alcoholics.

What is needed is for the Lord of Hosts to descend into those cellars, tip over the wine-racks, as He did the tables of the money-changers in the temple, and smash the bottles forever, letting their foul contents run down the sluices into Hell. He would like nothing better; all we have to do is open the cellar door and invite Him in.

Tito rode into Belgrade in the same open car as the Russian general in command of the liberating army. And once his Communists had secured their hold on Yugoslavia, the atrocities ceased, and order was restored. All Yugoslavia cheered when Tito stood up to Stalin. They cheered when he insisted on going his own way, and not becoming another puppet regime in the Warsaw Pact. They cheered louder, when he was excommunicated from the Cominform. But the cheering died away, as they realized that under Tito's Communism, life was really no different than what was taking place on the other side of their eastern borders.

One thing that Tito insisted upon, however, everyone agreed was a good thing: there would be no more ethnic strife whatever. Serbs and Croatians were to forget old scores and concentrate on becoming good Communists.

For the Serbs, this did not present a problem. Byzantine thinking had always regarded the State, in whatever form it took, as God's secular authority. They were comfortable with Communism, and the Serbian Orthodox Church, headquartered in Belgrade, soon reached an accommodation similar to the one arrived at in Moscow.

But the Croatians were another matter: the head of their church was in Rome, and he was implacably opposed to atheistic Communism. When Tito approached Cardinal Stepanic to persuade him that perhaps a more nationally-oriented Catholic Church might be appropriate for Yugoslavia, the latter categorically refused. And the Croatian people were no better; although there were many career opportunities in the new government—as teachers, administrators, civil servants or in the military—Croatians whose faith was important to them would not apply. Membership in the Communist Party was a requisite for advancement, and the Party denied the existence of God.

Occasionally Croatians did take government jobs—and faced a wry dilemma. In one town in Hercegovina, the parish priest came to the town officials to request that electricity be installed in his church.

"What do you need electricity for?" asked the local party leader. "Your services are all in the daytime."

"Yes," replied the pastor, "but those are for my believers.

It's your atheists who come secretly at night, to be married or have their children baptized."

It is comforting to think of Communism as a failed system, an intellectual aberration of the twentieth century that cannot recur, for the human race has grown too wise to be taken in again. It had captured the imagination of the downtrodden the world over, promising them equality and freedom; too late they discovered that they had merely exchanged one form of oppression for another. The few still ruled over the many. . . . and thus was the system doomed from the beginning.

But the reports of its demise are premature. There are still active Communist systems in the world, creaking and apathetic but far from imminent collapse. China, North Korea, North Viet Nam, Cuba—and Serbia, among others. Add to those, all the individualized variations on the Marxist-Leninist theme which might eschew the Communist label but fulfill all the criteria, and the number grows. And now, in the mother of them all, Russia, there is growing agitation for its return.

Not only is Communism far from moribund, but given its astonishing ability to mutate, in another generation we might have a whole new bag of isms that will seem fresh but will in actuality be all too familiar. It would behoove us, therefore, if we don't want our grandchildren to have to learn this lesson all over again, to look into the soul of Communism and see its fatal attraction. What made it so seductive? And how did it maintain its deadly grip, once it had charmed the hearts and the minds of the people?

The ultimate appeal of Communism—or of any system

which flattered the intellect—was the thing which put it into perpetual opposition to the Church. It explained why the two could never peacefully co-exist, and why the Church, merely by its existence, posed such a threat to Communism that it would do everything in its power to destroy it.

Communism's foundational tenet was that, at heart, man was good. Given enough time—and an equitable environment and the right incentives—his inherent goodness would rise to the surface. Each generation would be better than the one before, until paradise was achieved on earth. Man was good, and his goodness, given a chance, would produce more goodness. . . . Communism proposed to give him that chance.

The Church, on the other hand —the Body of Christ on earth—believed the exact opposite: Man, at heart, was a fallen creature. Ever since the first man and woman disobeyed God and fell from His grace, man had been inherently selfish. But the Creator was also the Forgiver. Man could turn back to God, and God would forgive him and dwell with him once again. If man chose to stay in close communion with his Creator, then he could usher in the Kingdom of God on earth—Paradise. The very thing that Communism ultimately promised.

The choice was man's. But to choose God's will over his own was often difficult. And to love God with all his heart and mind and soul and being, and to love his neighbor as himself, was to go totally against his nature. He could, however, be inspired. He could walk through the Red Sea, as if on dry land—and look back and see his oppressors foundering. He could see a prophet brought to his shores by a great fish which spat him out, so that he could call him to repent. . . .

But there came a time when man had so hardened his

heart against God, that he stoned God's prophets rather than listen to them. God loved him anyway—so much that He gave His only begotten Son, to show man the way to live, and to break forever the bondage of sin. Man was still naturally selfish—but he could be supernaturally inspired to selflessness. The Son had shown the way, the Holy Spirit had provided the means. The Kingdom of God could become reality on earth—but it meant choosing God in all things.

The first choice he faced, was to accept that he was a sinner, and therefore perpetually in need of God. That was where the Church and Communism were diametrically opposed, and why there could never be any ultimate reconciliation between the two. For Communism was like the second coming of the Serpent, whispering: "God is not telling you the truth: you are good! He does not want you to know it. He would have you believe that He is the only good one. Because if you know the truth, you will be like Him."

Communism (and every secular idealism) insisted that the Brotherhood of Man was not dependent upon the Fatherhood of God. Man needed no help from an imaginary divinity. All he needed was to live under a fair system, where all men had equal opportunity; then his innate goodness would bloom, as never before. *Fairness* was the touchstone by which all else would be measured.

Communism was born in an unfair world. On the continents of Europe and Asia, for centuries power had been gravitating into the hands of a very few—kings, emperors and czars who took great care to ensure that it would be passed on intact to their heirs. For their subjects, there was little chance of improving their lot in life. And even less chance of ever sharing in the power that the few held so tightly.

Their Christian faith was their only solace, and while it served them well, it did not seem to serve them as well as it did the Christians in America and subsequently Great Britain. There, a radical experiment in civil government, known as democracy and based on the model of the early Church, was flourishing. Democracy was not a natural system, for man was naturally selfish. In order to work, it depended on a measure of selflessness, for man had to voluntarily relinquish a portion of his personal rights, in order that his government might have the power to govern.

Voluntarily—that was the key. What it boiled down to was loving one's neighbor, and that could not happen without the continuing inspiration and subsequent morality of a strong, renewing faith. Democracy would never survive, where faith was not present.

The founding philosophers of Communism—Marx, Engels, Hegel—were insulted by the concept of God. Man had made God in his image, to comfort himself, an elaborate fantasy to help endure his miserable existence. "Religion is the opium of the people," wrote Karl Marx, as he envisioned a system in which such pathetic self-delusion would have no part. It was up to man to make his own world—the world God should have made but didn't. It would be, above all, a fair system, in which all men, regardless of birth, would be treated equally. No one would own more than his neighbor, and to ensure that, no one would own anything; everything would be held in common.

"From each according to his abilities, to each according to his needs"—Marx penned that phrase in 1875, and it became one of the founding tenets of Communism. It appealed to idealists everywhere, as well as to all who wanted what they did not have—and resented those who had more than they did.

The trouble was, there was a subtle flaw imbedded in this foundation: all men were *not* equal. They may have been *created* equal, all positioned on the same starting line, as democracy presupposed. But what happened after the starter's gun went off was a matter of genes, gifts, and individual motivation, and different individuals were differently motivated. Suppose a man worked twice as hard as the man next to him—was it fair to give the extra fruit of his labor to his lazy neighbor?

Solution: everything would be given to the State, and the State would re-apportion it to the people, as the State discerned their needs. Gradually the individual who was inclined to work hard, or who had unusual ability, realized that it was foolish to work harder than his neighbor. Initiative and incentive died.

But in the early years after World War II, when Communism was still attractive to the disenfranchised, and the first generation of idealists was still willing to sacrifice for the next, it could afford to be tolerant in victory. Christianity still existed in the USSR and the East Bloc countries. It was a remnant of the old system, espoused mostly by older believers. It was too late now to change their ways. But it was possible to make those ways extremely difficult.

Restrict their worship to churches, and close most of them. If their pastors objected, put them in prison. But do not close all the churches, or make unnecessary martyrs. Just let them know that they were being tolerated by a benevolent State which could, in an instant, put them all in prison, if provoked. When it came to intimidation—and every totalitarian system relied on fear to maintain order—it was seldom necessary to take the cudgel from the closet; a sidelong glance at the closet door was usually sufficient.

Pervasive fear was indispensable to the smooth functioning of a totalitarian state. Total control required massive doses of fear, frequently administered on all levels. It needed a comprehensive network of informants working with an invidious, ubiquitous secret police apparatus. Children should be encouraged to inform on their parents, teachers on their students, husbands on wives—everyone on everyone, up and down the social scale. No one should ever be entirely certain of the person to whom they were talking, or whether a third party might be listening on the phone.

The control had to be total, of course—because anything the State could not control, could become a problem. That was why Christianity was dangerous. Because if one truly believed in God, then one was not afraid of prison, or even death. And liquidation was the instrument of maximum intimidation.

So old Christians had to be handled with care—tolerated, harassed, even persecuted. But not driven too far. What Communism wanted was the next generation. When children saw how difficult life was for their Christian parents, that they would get nowhere in any job without joining the Communist Party, they would make the right decision. But the State had to work quickly on the little ones, before their minds could be poisoned. In grade school they were taught to pray to Lenin and Stalin, and their parents were forbidden to offer them any religious instruction. Violators could find themselves facing seven years' hard labor. This was true throughout the Soviet Union, and some East Bloc countries carried it even further: in Romania, for instance, it was the policy to take the young children of the devout, suddenly, without cause or warning, and place them in families far away, who could be counted on to raise them as good Communists.

In Yugoslavia, as elsewhere, the prevailing attitude was: let one more generation pass under Communism, and Christianity would be little more than a museum piece—an aberration which happened to produce some fine music and magnificent architecture, but an aberration, nonetheless.

And then, in the summer of 1981, six children in a remote mountain village in the province of Hercegovina, claimed to have seen the Mother of God.

Tolerance of Christians—the Party's policy was all well and good, when it came to old babushkas. It did no harm to let them go to their churches. But what was happening over in Medjugorje involved young *and* old—in fact, practically everyone in the 400 or so Croatian families that comprised that parish.

Alarming reports began arriving at the Government's local headquarters in nearby Citluk. According to those who made it their duty to keep the authorities informed, the six young people who claimed to have seen a divine vision returned to the site of the apparition the next afternoon—and saw it again! This time, they were accompanied by villagers. All claimed to have seen a glowing light, but only the six could see what was inside of it. The next afternoon, practically the entire village went with them, and the day after that, there were so many people on the hillside that their sources could not count them.

The situation was getting out of hand. The Croatians in this region were deeply religious; all but the most ambitious had steadfastly refused to have anything to do with Communism—even Tito's enlightened, progressive version of same. In the schools, the compulsory indoctrination had little impact on the children; they, like their parents, persisted in regarding the Communists as an occupying force. The only ones, young or old, who would cooperate were those for whom the local religion was not meaningful.

It almost made one question the wisdom of the Party's policy of tolerance. In other Communist countries, the Church had been given an ultimatum: cooperate or be shut down. In Albania the churches were closed, and in Bulgaria, the authorities were proud of their national atheism.

But in Yugoslavia, with its volatile mix of Muslims, Orthodox, and Roman Catholics, it was felt that harsh measures would pose a greater risk than tolerance. Handling religion was like handling unstable explosives— you did so with extreme caution. Especially the Croatians— four centuries of ruthless Turkish oppression, bent on the systematic eradication of their faith, had only succeeded in driving it underground—and making it the most important element of their lives. It still was.

Modern Communism had become more enlightened, however; it had learned that it was counter-productive to drive the Church into hiding. Better to keep it on the surface, where one could keep track of its members and their whereabouts. Anyone mistaking tolerance for naivete, however, did so at their peril: the State still regarded the Church as potentially its greatest problem. Where the proletariat was concerned, the State could control everything—even, to some extent, people's minds. But it could not control their hearts.

Normally that was not a problem: man's heart being

basically selfish, the right application of fear and greed would achieve the desired results. (The Communist hierarchy had no illusions about the goodness of man. That might be useful for recruiting foreign intelligentsia, but modern Communism owed much of its rapid growth to the fact that its leaders were hard-eyed realists.) What made man's natural instinct toward selfishness so useful was that it was insatiable. In the West, under capitalism, where one could keep what one acquired, one could never acquire enough. In the beginning, it was things—to make life more bearable, then comfortable and enjoyable. But eventually it was simply money, and the control it could buy.

In the Communist East, money was not the goal. But control was. And the further one rose, the more control he could exercise over his environment, his future, and eventually over those around him. This last was power—and power, the Communist leadership knew, was the ultimate incentive. It was addictive: once a man developed a taste for it, he would do anything to obtain more—or hold on to that which he already had.

Moreover, the attraction of power worked on all levels. The local commissar would do exactly as his superiors wished, because he enjoyed the power his position afforded him. The most insignificant bureaucrat relished his or her authority, however limited or transient. At an airport, for instance, regardless of how highly-regarded or influential a traveler might be anywhere else, when he or she stood at the counter, for that moment they were completely at the mercy of the official opposite them.

As with many narcotics, the addiction to power was exponential; the more one had, the more one had to have. And when he had obtained all there was to obtain, it drove him mad.

Lord Acton was correct: power did tend to corrupt, and absolute power tended to corrupt absolutely. In the modern era, in terms of life and death, Stalin had accrued more power than anyone, even Hitler. Yet his last years were spent in a twilight of raging paranoia. Reminiscent of Herod of old, he carried out purge after purge of his officer corps, in the hope of eliminating anyone who might one day lead a coup against him.

As useful as selfishness was in motivating individuals, it was even more effective in motivating men corporately. There, you had peers affirming to one another that what they were doing was right and justified by history, their patriotic duty, in fact. When a nation coveted a neighbor's land or mineral or industrial resources, a suitable pretext for invasion could always be found. "We are going there at the invitation of the local government, to restore order (or maintain peace, or protect our countrymen who are in the minority there)."

Whether the *Panzerkorps* was rolling into the Sudetenland for the sake of *Liebensraum* or the Rhineland or Austria, it was always with the noblest of intent. On the border of Poland, on September 1, 1939, the Nazis staged a mock attack against their own positions. The finer points of motivation could even be worked out afterwards, as long as they were soon broadcast far and wide. As Joseph Goebbels, Hitler's genius of propaganda, explained: a lie repeated often enough becomes the truth. And even if it is not wholly or widely believed, it can still fulfill its purpose. Those who were inclined to believe it, would; in the minds of those who were not inclined, doubt would be sown. You did not have to convince those who would oppose you; all you had to do was cause them to hesitate. As they paused, you moved. And by the time they collected their resolve, it would be too late.

The world would always believe what it wanted to believe. And the world, like the individual, was selfish. Not wanting to intervene on behalf of the threatened, given half an excuse not to, it wouldn't. In the late Thirties, Dr. Goebbels correctly gauged how badly the world wanted to preserve peace—enough to allow itself to be convinced that National Socialism's appetite for land and conquest could be appeased.

If a nation were strong enough, and its assessment of the free world's resolve (or lack of it) accurate enough, it could even afford to ignore world opinion. When the tanks with the red stars rolled into Budapest in '56 and Prague in '68, they accurately anticipated that the West would not become involved in a land war in Europe, regardless of what the Voice of America might have led the freedom fighters to believe. And when the free world subsequently censured their brutal repression, they insisted that they were responding to the appeals of government authorities (which they neglected to name) to restore order, maintain peace, and protect the minority of Soviet citizens. Having weighed negative world opinion against the goals of holding onto Hungary and Czechoslovakia (and setting an example for restive elements in other East Bloc countries), they had decided that it was worth the risk. In time, the world's objections would die away.

As long as a man remained selfish at heart, he could be controlled. And that was why the Church would always be Communism's most dangerous interior adversary. Because the Church inspired selflessness in the hearts of men. Those who firmly believed in the myth of God, that they were created by a loving Father who heard their prayers, began to behave in an unpredictable way. They stopped caring about acquiring control—and started caring for their neighbors. They could no longer be moved by the carrot—and began to lose their fear of the stick.

In short, they began doing freely and spontaneously what Communism had been unable to force its followers to do in seventy years: those who were able, began helping those who were not. When Jesus gave His followers the second Great Commandment—to love their neighbors as themselves—He was saying essentially the same thing as Marx. The difference was, the response to the former was spontaneous, to the latter coerced. *From each according to his abilities, to each according to his needs. . . .*

Coups could be countered, resistance movements infiltrated, uprisings crushed. But an undivided heart, once committed, could not be turned. When a man could no longer be ruled by fear of torture or imprisonment, or of death itself, then by his mere existence he became a threat to the State.

It mattered not that he submitted to civil authority, or that he prayed for his enemies and counseled peace. That he existed at all would inspire others. He would become a rallying point; his faith would be emulated, and would spread and deepen, until you had a whole populace no longer controllable.

Whenever a totalitarian state went to war, therefore, as it conquered territory, its first priority was to subdue the Church. If that meant destroying a house of worship, regardless of its age or value as a cultural monument, then so be it. If it meant driving off—or killing—its pastor, then so be it. They might not be able to kill God, but they could erase the physical evidence of His presence.

In the offices of the Provincial in Mostar, there is an ancient volume bound in crumbling black leather. This is *The Book of the Dead.* In it is recorded the death of each Franciscan priest—the date, the place, and the circumstances. With the invasion of the Nazis in 1941, the entries suddenly escalate, and the causes of death are no longer natural: "machine-gunned on the steps of his church" or "executed in the public square" or "drowned in the Neretva River."

When the grey wolf was finally driven out by the red wolf, the rate of entries increases. On many lines the dates are only approximate, and there are no places or circumstances listed; no one knew where or how they died—only that they were gone.

But in peacetime, such measures were seldom necessary. Even in Hercegovina, where the concentration of Roman Catholics was the densest (in population, Serbs, Croatians, and Muslims were roughly equal), and their faith ran deep, the people had remained tractable enough. Indeed, until these open-air, mass demonstrations began on June 25, 1981, nothing out of the ordinary had taken place. And so far, these gatherings had been peaceful—but all it would take would be one firebrand, and they could have a major problem on their hands. In Poland, the Solidarity Movement was gaining strength; if it ever got into the minds of the people here that they might protest. . . .

Something had to be done, and quickly, or higher authorities in Mostar, the capital of Hercegovina, would be demanding an explanation.

The local Communists took action. Rounding up the six young people, they brought them to the police station, where they were interrogated extensively and then examined by a doctor. To the authorities' dismay, he pronounced them normal and healthy—which gave them no alternative but to release them.

Next, they summoned Medjugorje's Franciscan pastor, Father Jozo Zovko, and informed him that the apparitions must cease. That priest would have liked nothing more. But he himself had interviewed the six children at length, and he knew their families; as far as he could discern, they were not perpetrating a hoax, nor had they become trapped into perpetuating what had started as a childish prank. Whatever was happening, the children were convinced it was real.

In that case, concluded the authorities, they were either experiencing mass hallucination or were psychologically unbalanced—or both. (It was out of the question that they were telling the truth. If God did not exist, neither did His mother.)

Now they dispatched a state psychiatrist, Dr. Darinka Glamuzina, to the scene. She could be relied upon to discredit the phenomenon. But after observing the children at close quarters during the next apparition, she descended the hill visibly shaken and subsequently refused to file a report.

To make matters worse, they were now receiving reports of miraculous healings—a paralyzed child was walking, a blind man's sight had been restored. People were leaving their jobs to be present on the hillside, and the roads were jammed with cars, some whose license plates indicated they had come more than a hundred kilometers to be there! The authorities shuddered; never mind Mostar! They would soon be hearing from Sarajevo!

The children had to be mentally deranged, they reasoned, and now the authorities took them to the neuro-psychiatric department of the state hospital in Mostar. Surely there. . . . But once again the children were found to be of sound mind and body, and were returned to their homes.

The psychiatric field, which had served the USSR so well in dealing with its own hard-core dissidents, was proving useless. But if modern science could not arrive at a rational explanation, what else was there?

They decided to try one more time. Two Government social workers, known to the children, offered to take them on a day of sightseeing. The young people accepted, and off they went. But as the time of the apparition approached, they asked to return to the hill. The social workers just kept driving. Finally the children threatened to jump out of the car, if they didn't stop. The car pulled over, the children got out, and at the time of the apparition all of them (including the social workers) saw a bright ball of light approaching from the direction of the hill. Kneeling by the roadside, the children saw the apparition, and the next day the social workers resigned their positions with the Government and moved to another district.

That did it: the authorities banned all further open-air gatherings. If the children wanted to make fools of themselves, they could do so in the church—but out of sight, so that they would not make fools of others. It did no good; it just meant the church was now packed every afternoon.

They tried threatening the visionaries, as they were now being called. And these were no idle threats; with the Government controlling everything, including work permits, the visionaries' families could be made to suffer grievously. But the apparitions continued.

In desperation, the authorities demanded that the pastor close the church. He refused—and was soon arrested and charged with spreading sedition. He went to prison for a year and a half at hard labor.

Immediately after his arrest, the church was vandalized, and the authorities ordered it closed. The people ignored the order, and that same afternoon, after the Mass, there was an apparition during the rosary, in the little sacristy, adjacent to the altar. At the end of it, the youngest visionary, little Jacov, came out and told the people that the Blessed Mother was pleased with them and not to be afraid, and that she would protect Father Jozo.

The authorities now faced a quandary: if they forcibly closed the church, they might well incite the very uprising they were anxious to avoid. Reluctantly they returned to the Government's original policy of tolerance. The apparitions would be permitted to continue (since they seemed powerless to prevent them), but it would be under continuing surveillance and harassment.

The intimidation tactics extended to the pilgrims who had begun to arrive in significant numbers. If, as they entered the country, they displayed any Bibles or religious articles, these would be confiscated. Outdoor gatherings were prohibited, and police cars patrolled the area. Overhead, helicopters could appear at any hour, and were known to hover noisily over the church during services. The Government was making it abundantly clear to the pilgrims that their presence was not appreciated.

Then suddenly, after seven years of such harassment, the Government belatedly realized just how much money— hard foreign currency—the pilgrims were spending. Medjugorje had become one of the major sources of tourist revenue, not just in Bosnia-Hercegovina, but in all Yugoslavia! For many were coming in through Belgrade and flying on JAT...

Abruptly the Government reversed its position. While still officially disapproving of the apparitions, the Communists now joined the race to build accommodations. One could easily tell which of the new hotels going up were being built by Communists; they were the ones on which construction continued through the afternoon Masses and all day Sundays.

So things proceeded, until the national referendum of 1989 when Communism in Yugoslavia caved in, as it had in so many other East Bloc countries. For the next halcyon year and a half, Medjugorje blossomed in the sun, enjoying freedom like it had never known. Pilgrims poured in. The building boom struggled to keep pace. A beautiful stone plaza now stretched before the church, and a long row of outdoor confessionals was erected to handle all those anxious to be reconciled with God. The road to the church was widened and resurfaced, to allow the huge tour buses to pass one another. Behind the church, a white outdoor altar was constructed in the round (locals fondly nicknamed it "the Gazebo"), to handle the huge overflow crowds.

To the pilgrims it appeared that life could only get better for Medjugorje; indeed, some now feared that the villagers' new prosperity might harm them spiritually. Expensive foreign cars appeared—with local license plates. And families who formerly could barely afford meat once a week, now had color television sets.

But in distant Belgrade, things were far from peaceful. With the sudden removal of the system which had suppressed their differences for forty-five years, the six republics were finding they had little in common. Serbia, the largest, and Montenegro, its ally, maintained their allegiance to the former system and to its Communist leaders. But Slovenia and Croatia, given a taste of democracy, were now agitating for complete independence. Macedonia was not yet ready to sever ties, and neither was Bosnia-Hercegovina, with its mix of Muslims, Orthodox, and Croatians. In the interim, to maintain civil authority in Yugoslavia, they cobbled together a rotating presidency, with a representative from each republic taking his turn. To this factionalized and increasingly tenuous civil authority, the federal army paid grudging subservience.

All of which was of little concern to pilgrims on their way to Medjugorje. After all, it was an old ethnic animosity, wasn't it? The Serbs and the Croatians had never gotten along—the bad blood probably went all the way back to Constantine, or even before. And then, just to make it more complicated, you had all those Muslims. . . .

Of more immediate concern to visiting pilgrims was whether their bus would reach the village in time for the Croatian Mass—which was as it should be—they were on a pilgrimage, coming for spiritual not geo-political understanding. And with all the things on their must-see, must-do lists, they could be forgiven if making sense of the political ferment seething about them was not one of them.

All that would change in a single day: June 25, 1991. Suddenly, there on America's evening news, was the Yugoslav Army, using planes and tanks to keep Slovenia and Croatia from leaving the federation.

As the war news from Yugoslavia worsened, friends of Medjugorje now began to receive reports of churches being deliberately destroyed. At first, it was incomprehensible; they must be random casualties, regrettable but inevitable in a combat zone. But when the coastal city of Split came under bombardment, its cathedral was hit from eight different directions. . . .

As town after town came under attack, it was repeatedly reported that one of the gunners' first targets was the local church. The toll of churches thus destroyed reached 64, then 102, then 284, then 350. There was nothing random about this, and upon reflection, it could be seen why. The federal army remained the strongest single element in the crumbling federation. Yugoslavia might not survive, but the army would. Its general staff and officer corps consisted almost exclusively of hard-line Communists. As such, they would regard the Church as their most dangerous long-term enemy.

What relation did this bear to Medjugorje? The little Croatian village in the mountains of Hercegovina was the source of the greatest renewal and inspiration which the Church in Yugoslavia (and many other places) had received in modern times. The pilgrimages may have stopped, but the inspiration continued. As long as that light was allowed to shine, it posed a threat to the darkness.

Anticipating the republic of Bosnia-Hercegovina's tilt towards independence and the hostilities which were likely to ensue, the federal army had long ago begun stockpiling. The greatest problem facing an army of conquest in mountainous terrain was the vulnerability of its supply lines. In that eventuality, the army now had enough supplies of all kinds around Mostar to be entirely self-sufficient. And to ensure a favorable outcome of any hostilities, it had summoned thousands of reservists, paramilitary irregulars, and civilian "freedom fighters" to join it in Mostar. They were there to maintain order and preserve peace and protect minorities.

Meanwhile, everyone was arming themselves and preparing for the worst. The region around Medjugorje had become a tinder-dry forest. If it ignited, the subsequent holocaust would make all that had happened in Croatia seem pale in comparison.

10

The War of Words

The 1989 referendum sounded the death knell of Communist Yugoslavia. Immediately Slovenia and Croatia opened negotiations to achieve their independence. For when Tito had created the new Yugoslavia, he had guaranteed that each of the six republics who were joining the federation of their own free will and volition, was free to leave at any time. He could afford to be so magnanimous, since the only legitimate political party in each republic was the Communist Party, and there was no chance that the regional Communists would ever allow their republics to leave. But now they had voted themselves out of existence.

Chaos ensued. The solution was a rotating presidency, with elected representatives from each republic taking turns in the top office. But when it came the turn of the representative from Croatia, Serbian officials maneuvered to block him from taking office. They also stalled all negotiations for independence and mounted a massive campaign to convince Western Europe and the U.S. that the surviving Communists were struggling to preserve stability in Yugoslavia, and prevent the ethnic unrest that was already erupting in the USSR and elsewhere.

That struck a responsive chord. In the wake of Communism's demise, the thing old hands in the State Department and the British Foreign Office feared the most was that the long-suppressed nationalism of all those peoples would now re-surface—with a vengeance. And vengeance was the right word: many of these peoples, with large cellars stocked with vintage hatred, had been biding their time. . . . In the old diplomats' worst-case scenario, civilization on the Continent would disintegrate into a rabble of quarreling mini-nations. With a shudder, they referred to it as "the tribalization of Europe"—and saw it as a descent into a new Dark Age.

The surviving Communists had a second card to play: Slovenia and Croatia had both been part of the old Austro-Hungarian Empire, and during World War II, the Croatians had sided with Hitler. (They neglected to mention that more Croatians had fought against fascism than with it.) Which nations today, they asked, were most sympathetic to the break-away republics' bid for independence? Austria, Germany, and Italy. Did the British and the French—and the U.S.—really want two more nations aligning themselves with these old Axis Powers? Or with the new Germany, which was emerging as the dominant member of the European Community?

Seeing that they had scored on both points, the Serbian Communists now played to that fear. And they were playing with a loaded deck: all of Yugoslavia's diplomats, who for years had been cultivating Western friendships through all of their embassies and consulates, were Serbian Communists. So were all of their communications personnel, providing liaison for Western media. And so were all of the heads of the different ministries and departments and agencies with whom Western businessmen had to deal. Even the people employed by the U.S. Embassy in Belgrade were Serbian Communists.

There were two elements, however, over which the Serbian Communists could exercise no spin control: the Church, and modern technology.

As always, the Church was the main enemy. And the Church was doing what it could to balance the picture that the West was getting. As hostilities broke out in Croatia, and the federal army began to roll, the Church got the word out that its churches, monasteries and convents were being systematically targeted for destruction.

The Communists tried to blunt the effectiveness of this effort, knowing that the outcome of the struggle in Croatia would ultimately be decided in the court of world opinion. And that the crucial weapon in such an arena was not truth, but perceived truth—in other words, propaganda. They insisted that the Catholic Church was in league with the Croatians and could not be trusted as an objective source. They were certainly not mentioning the atrocities being committed by Croatian extremists. (And some were occurring, according to Western journalists.) For every claim of Communist wrong-doing, they made the exact same counter-claim, calculating that the world, not knowing which side to believe, would withhold judgment.

But as the number of destroyed churches and cultural monuments mounted, they began resorting to desperate measures. In the town of Sid, on the border between Slavonia and Serbia, they went so far as to shell an Orthodox church, and then claim that it had been done by Croatians. The trouble was, the town was on the Serbian side of the border, and there were no Croatian forces anywhere in

Serbia (and few anywhere else, with tanks or heavy artillery). In fact, at no time had there been aggression from west to east; only from east to west.

This was a new wrinkle on an old Communist tactic. In the final days of World War II in Yugoslavia, as the tide of battle reached the hilltop Franciscan monastery of Siroki Brijeg (where Father Jozo is now on the faculty), an advance party killed the twelve friars who were still there. Then donning the dead priests' robes, from highly-visible upper windows and towers they fired on the main body of their approaching comrades, before throwing off the robes and disappearing. In the war of propaganda, perceived truth was all that mattered; word spread far and wide of Franciscans shooting at Partisans. (This incident is related in detail in Father Svet's book, *Pilgrimage.*)

Modern technology, however, was a Communist nightmare. Fax machines could relay written stories and photographs instantaneously, and satellite up-links enabled live television coverage of anything, anywhere. The world had become a global village, with everyone able to look in everyone else's window. But perhaps the greatest single advance in the cause of protecting human rights was the invention of the handheld videocamera. Eyewitness accounts could be discredited, audiotapes could be dubbed, still photographs could be posed or faked or doctored. But it was virtually impossible to alter truth captured on videotape.

And now videotapes of mutilated victims were being smuggled out of Croatian war zones—smuggled, because the federal army was restricting all Western journalists and E.C. monitoring teams from such zones. They claimed it was "for their own safety," and nineteen journalists who defied that order were indeed killed (no one knows by whom). The generals had all seen the live video coverage from Tiananmen Square in Beijing, where Chinese students had stood up to tanks, and they had noted the profound effect of such footage on the rest of the world. They wanted to ensure that whatever was occurring under their command would remain hidden.

But now, despite the ban, somehow, someone was getting videotapes of horribly mutilated bodies out. What had been done in darkness, was being shouted from the housetops.

The Communists stepped up their propaganda campaign, though now there was an edge of panic in their pronouncements. Among the Croatians, there was a lunatic fringe of ultra-nationalists. Proud to be called Ustase, they committed pay-back atrocities and said the sort of things that Communists could offer as proof that the Croatians were a genocidal race. The implication was that the Communists, by seeking to systematically annihilate the Croatians and their culture were doing the world a favor. And more than a few in the West, predisposed to believe the worst about Croatians, would privately nod their heads—just as more than a few had privately believed that Hitler was doing the world a favor by ridding it of Jews.

It did not matter to the Communists that the West was not being won over by their arguments or even impressed that there was much truth in them. They had caused the West to pause. Despite growing evidence that a horror of monumental proportions was taking place in Croatia, despite frantic appeals that the West at least level the playing field and allow Croatians to buy modern weapons to defend themselves against the latest tanks and planes, the European Community did little. And the United States, making a great show of deferring to their lead, did even less.

Had the U.S. gone strongly on record as opposing any further war of conquest, Belgrade might have paused. And reflected. And decided that perhaps they should be satisfied with what they had gained. But the U.S. said nothing. The propaganda had done its work.

When the E.C. imposed sanctions on all the republics, the U.S. followed suit. Wishful thinkers thought: if we shut off their oil, sooner or later their tanks will grind to a halt and their planes will be grounded. But they had not considered the federal army's long-range strategy. Against just such a contingency, the army had laid up nearly a year's supply of fuel. The tanks kept rolling.

In the name of fairness, the West had adopted a hands-off policy towards what was happening in Yugoslavia. Said one State Department official who preferred to remain nameless, the hatred between Serb and Croat ran so deep "that if we took away their guns, they'd only go at each other with knives."

But as it played out, the non-intervention doctrine proved less than fair. It would be one thing if both parties were of equal strength and equally interested in pursuing peace. But if one was behaving like a schoolyard bully, then non-intervention sent an unmistakable signal: it was all right for the bully to keep on doing what he was doing. The only thing he understood was the threat of superior force. If the one being picked on had an older brother who was willing to come to the schoolyard, the bully would leave him alone. And since bullies were cowards at heart, it was seldom necessary for the older brother to actually appear; the possibility that he might was sufficient. The West's non-intervention policy was telling the Communists that Croatia had no older brother.

Finally, in January of this year, Germany decided it could no longer look the other way. When they declared that they would recognize Slovenia and Croatia alone, if

necessary, to stop the war, the rest of Europe hastened
to do likewise. Seeing their success, Bosnia-Hercegovina
and Macedonia now began agitating for independence, too.
And even Montenegro began to have doubts about the
wisdom of remaining inextricably linked to Serbia.

In America, those sympathetic to Croatia's plight wrote
letters to their Congressmen and to newspapers, they called
or faxed anybody they knew personally who might have
any influence in Washington, but still their government
did nothing. They wondered why—unwilling to believe that
the only reason the Bush administration had moved so
swiftly and resolutely to the defense of Kuwait, was because
of that nation's oil. Kuwait was not even a democracy, they
argued, and Croatia's independence had been legitimately
and democratically obtained. Were we really so callous?
But if we weren't, why had we lagged so far behind Europe,
in helping the Kurdish refugees in northern Iraq? Surely
that was one time we should have led, instead of followed.
And now that the E.C. had recognized Slovenia and Croatia,
how long would the U.S. hesitate? Would they be the 34th
in line, as they were in recognizing Lithuania?

By the end of February, the President was wholly pre-
occupied with the forthcoming primaries. It was ironic that
the very political sensitivity which was distracting the
President now, might work in Bosnia-Hercegovina's favor
later. This was an election year, and two million Croatian-
American voters would be going to the ballot box in the
fall. Add to that number the eight or nine million American
voters whose lives had been touched by Medjugorje. . . .

Tragically, by the time the President realized how large
a block of votes might be involved, it could be too late.
In a few more weeks, it might be all over.

11

The Leviathan

The great imponderable continued to be the federal army. Until now, it had paid grudging lip-service to the shared civilian authority in Belgrade. But with the departure of Slovenia and Croatia, that authority had become even more of a charade. The man calling the shots was the Serbian president, Slobodan Milosevic, and he was in a hurry. The cards had been dealt, but the hand must be played quickly; there was no telling how much longer the window to achieve Greater Serbia would remain open. Were Milosevic ever to reverse course and wholeheartedly embrace the peace process, the ultra-nationalists would cast him aside.

And if they didn't, the army might well turn on him and rend him. One had the picture of a man walking a large, menacing guard dog; as long as they were both going in the same direction, it was fine. But the dog, not the man, decided in which direction they would go next.

The army, the third largest land force in Europe, was so massive and had been in place so long that it had become a *de facto* government unto itself, a state within the state. Its generals were all old, hard-line Communists, but there was nothing old about the army itself. The generals had insisted on regularly modernizing and upgrading their equipment, and the civilian government had meekly complied. As a result, the federal army had the best hardware that the USSR had been willing to let the nations of the Warsaw Pact have. (It was not the *very* best hardware; the Red Army reserved that for itself. Allies were allies, but in the Communist system, you learned never to trust anyone completely; Stalin had taught that, and Stalin was right. The Soviet leaders were realists: they knew that the people under them were disaffected. Even so, Russians could be relied on to obey orders. But what of Czechs? Poles? Yugoslavs? In the unlikely event of a counter-revolution, the Red Army's tanks and Migs had better be one generation newer.)

The federal army in Yugoslavia was far better equipped than the Croatian defenders they faced who, with the exception of the equipment of units they had been able to persuade to join them, were by and large making do with World War II vintage small arms and hunting rifles. Nor was that equation soon likely to change: E.C. recognition had not ended the arms embargo. It was a come-as-you-are war, and the federal army, whose *raison d'etre* was the defense of Yugoslavia in the event the red wolf should ever turn south, had put a high priority on preparedness. It was ready for this war. Add to that, the white-piece advantage—of being the one to decide where and when the next action would be fought, plus vast numerical superiority, total mobility, and modern communications. . . . On paper, the federal army was invincible.

But wars were never fought on paper. At the outset, a war's tactics and strategy might follow the textbooks written on the previous war, but the side which could best improvise and innovate would soon gain an inestimable advantage. The annals of military history are lined with the campaigns of great innovators. Caesar, Washington, Forest, Lee, Lawrence, Rommel, Wingate, MacArthur, Schwartzkopf— each seemed to know exactly what his opposite number was thinking, and how he would respond. It was as if they were eavesdropping on their staff meetings. . . .

Under the Communist system, however, original thinking was not encouraged; innovative leaders, military or civilian—were leaders who might one day be a problem, might even pose a threat to the system. Innovators seldom attained strategy-formulating rank. Advancement instead went to the politically attuned, the competent, the capable, the grey. While the federal army of Yugoslavia's long-range planning and preparedness could not be faulted, their battlefield tactics were singularly uninspired. The reduction of Vukovar had taken three times as long as anticipated. The assault on Dubrovnik was so full of blunders and miscalculations, it must have been embarrassing. And when the army's top generals found themselves thrust into the exceedingly uncomfortable limelight before international television cameras, they were uniformly lackluster and colorless.

But no matter how daring or innovative the Croatian resistance might seem in contrast, nor how highly motivated their troops, in the end courage and inspiration might not be enough to affect the outcome. For the army's leadership, though grey, was also highly motivated. The senior commissioned officers and reservists were all professionals whose pay scale was far above what they could earn in civilian life, and who could count on large pensions when they finally retired—so large, in fact, that they would be able to live more comfortably than most men their age still working. And as they were nearly all Serbian, this disparity would be even more pronounced in that impoverished republic.

The bulk of the army, however, was still made up of draftees. These were still being drawn from the four republics still remaining in the rump-state of Yugoslavia, though non-Serbian desertions were running extremely high—especially since new recruits were invariably the first troops sent into combat, to draw fire and reveal enemy positions. As a result, the draft was less than 15% successful, despite the death penalty for evasion.

But at the senior commissioned and non-commissioned levels, and among the reservists, morale remained high— albeit enormously expensive. Their exorbitant salaries and pensions, to say nothing of the maintenance of all that sophisticated hardware, was part of the reason why the army consumed an incredible 70% of the gross national product—and that was *before* (and part of the reason *why*) Slovenia and Croatia had broken away. These two republics, with 38% of Yugoslavia's population, had been contributing 55% of the GNP.

Such simple, unequivocal economics helped to explain why the army had supported Milosevic, as he claimed to be trying to hold Yugoslavia together. Why they had stockpiled so heavily in the Mostar area. And why so many reservists had responded so readily to the army's call to join them there. If Bosnia-Hercegovina were allowed to follow Slovenia and Croatia, it was possible that the GNP would lose another 20%.

This also explained why the army had no interest in

pursuing peace. If peace were ever to become permanent, and these highly-paid professionals were deactivated, they would go home to—nothing. For more than forty years, this had not been a problem; the threat of the massive Soviet Red Army was enough to silence anyone who questioned how much their own army was costing. But suddenly, to the dumbfoundment of the Yugoslav army's generals, that threat had—vanished.

They needed an immediate reason to continue to exist, and they settled on peace-keeping—even if it meant they had to foment the unrest which they then moved in to quell. As Croatian resistance stiffened, they became the necessary threat. But the matter had to be decided soon; the army was about to bankrupt what was left of Yugoslavia.

III

The Present

12

December in Mostar

After breakfast Tuesday morning (December 10), the editor went back over to Mostar. Father Svet had arranged an interview with Milivoj Gagro, the mayor of that beleaguered city, and as he accompanied his friend to the municipal offices, he said, "You will like this man. It is a hard job—impossible, under these circumstances. But even his political opponents admit that he is doing as well as anyone could."

They were joined by Father Svet's cousin, Jozo Kraljevic, who would act as interpreter. A former history teacher who was now in the import-export business, he had acted as interpreter for visiting BBC television productions, and had also done the English translation of Father Slavko's first book, *Pray with the Heart.*

The mayor was a broad-shouldered, square-jawed man, graying at the temples, with a twinkle in his eye. He took his time responding to the questions, though he was quick to understand them.

Who exactly were the soldiers that seemed to be everywhere in the streets? There were actually two military presences in the vicinity of Mostar—the federal army, headquartered in Trebinje to the southeast, and five to eight thousand reservists from Serbia and Montenegro on the outskirts of the city, plus civilian irregulars. The Army Corps of the 2nd Operating Zone consisted of 20,000 federal troops, and it was these who were waging war up and down the coast, and laying siege to Dubrovnik. The reservists had come on the 20th of September.

Why were they here? The status of the republic of Bosnia-Hercegovina had yet to be defined. In the event that it should go independent, they were here ostensibly to safeguard the Serbian minority; approximately 19% of the regional population was Serbian.

Had there been instances of persecution to these Serbs? "No, not a single one. Not in forty years."

Sunday night, parked in front of the Hotel Ruja, were two white Peugeot jeeps, each with a circle of blue stars on its door—were these the vehicles of the European Community monitoring team? The Mayor nodded. Had they been able to help? "We asked the E.C's to ask the commander of the army to set forth any factors which have led them to conclude there could be ethnic conflicts here. But they have refused to speak on this subject, either to the E.C. or to us." He added that a few days before, the head of the E.C. mission, in Sarajevo, after many attempts was able to establish contact with the commanding officer at Trebinje. "On his way there, he stopped here, and I told him: If we want peace, and they want peace, the only way to achieve it is by our talking."

What was the response? Mayor Gagro sighed; there was none.

What about the U.N.? "If the blue helmets come, I think

all our problems are solved. Then there will be peace, and the army and reservists will have no more reason to stay."

How likely was their coming? The mayor shrugged. "They have stipulated that there must first be peace, and then they must be welcomed by all parties; the SDS (the Serbian Democratic Party) doesn't want them." Why? Because they wanted a solution that favored the Serbs—a supervised, democratic solution would not do that. They comprised barely a fifth of Mostar's 126,000 population, yet here, as elsewhere, they held four-fifths of the government and civil service positions.

What if the blue helmets did not come? The mayor thought for a moment. "Less than a month ago, thirty communes, mostly in Hercegovina, presented a manifesto which declared that we supported a sovereign and independent Bosnia-Hercegovina—within existing borders. But if we are forced to join Greater Serbia, the Croatian people would never agree to it." And should Serbia insist? "Then," he said sadly, "there will be war."

Were the sanctions having any effect? The mayor looked out the window. When a people's future was at stake, such things as no benzine were of little consequence. This was a land of scanty soil, he explained; earning a living from it was difficult. But it made a strong people, a people used to enduring deprivation. It also made them strong in spirit. "Over here, a man has his dignity," he declared. "He is never going to give that away for some secondary human needs. What he must do without for the moment, means nothing when measured against eternity. He will do what he must, for future generations."

And if the blue helmets did not come? "Our man will not attack anybody. But he is ready to defend himself."

On another subject, what about refugees? America was

receiving reports of up to half a million Croatians forced from their homes or fleeing cities and towns under attack. Most were going further into Croatia—were any coming here? The mayor again referred to the typical Slav: he was self-reliant, resourceful, unused to accepting help from anyone. Most of the refugees simply went to relatives; very few went to the Red Cross or official relief organizations. During World War II, when so many families had been uprooted ahead of the Partisans, there was a large transient population. Many new friendships were made then, sharing good and evil—and so it is, today.

Exactly how many refugees would he say were in Mostar, right now? "About 600 have registered. But they stay only a short time, before going on their way. People do not linger in places which they feel are not appropriate for them."

Many Americans, despite their government's official policy, were anxious to help. Even as they spoke, large clothing drives were underway—was that what they needed most? The mayor shook his head. Clothing was no problem; their own charitable agencies were meeting that need. And food? "Food is a problem. Normally we would buy our food from Serbia and Croatia—but those borders are closed now." How critical was the situation? "We have enough food for another month—maybe two, if we cut down to subsistence level. Then we will be in real trouble." Medical supplies? He smiled. "A large shipment just arrived from England. The doctors are very happy."

That left heating fuel—the Ruja, for instance, had none. Now the mayor beamed. "We have the Neretva. Up above here, it is very mountainous—very good for hydro-electric power plants. When the sanctions cut off our oil, we suddenly had so much rain, the river was always full! Thanks to God's help, we have been able to compensate for heating oil with electricity."

Then food was the thing they needed most from their American friends? "No. The food will only allow us to exist. It is more important to remain free. Ask your friends to ask your politicians and President Bush to intercede. We have our dignity and do not like having to beg for food. All we want is the chance to work and live in peace, with dignity."

The American people would do everything they could, he was assured, but if it was not enough— The mayor took a deep breath. "Over this city, which I love, there is a black cloud which could rain terrible misery. In our local parliament, we have adopted a declaration that Mostar is a demilitarized zone, an open city, in accordance with international law." He paused. "But if America does not intercede, then one night, on your evening news, you will see another city being destroyed. It won't be Vukovar, or Dubrovnik. It will be Mostar."

13

No Place to Lay
One's Head

The refugee family was alone in the dormitory bedroom, sitting on chairs at the end of a long row of bunks. It was a little after noon, and the tall windows made the room bright and cheery; the little family, however—father, mother, son, daughter-in-law, and little granddaughter— looked forlorn. Their story was so exactly like the stories of a hundred thousand other dispossessed Croatian families, it would stand for all. [Their names have been changed to protect their relatives; everything else is verbatim.]

The father, Ivan, had short iron-gray hair and a face that was seamed from years of driving a tractor in the sun. His frame was blunt and blocky, and his hands were hardened with callouses. He could smile, but not readily. Ivan was 54 and looked ten years older; he did the talking for the family.

They had all lived together on the family farm in the town of Tovarnik, which was in Slavonia, just inside the

Croatian border, about 12 kilometers south of the Danube, or Dunav, as it was called in Serbia. It was a modest farm, on which they grew mostly wheat. But unlike the mountainous regions of the rest of Croatia, the soil on those plains was extraordinarily fertile—Slavonia was known as the bread-basket of Yugoslavia—and one could do quite well on even a modest farm. After they had turned in their wheat harvest to the collective, what they were allowed to keep was enough to feed *ten* families. What they did not need for themselves, they were allowed to take to market. As a result, they had two tractors with trailers, a harvester, a combine, and all the necessary accessories to make this equipment complete. They also had a nice house, a car, six pigs weighing 200 kilos each (440 lbs), and some goats.

The farm had been in their family for at least four generations—maybe longer. Ivan didn't know; when he was a little boy, his grandfather once told him that he, too, as a little boy, had grown up on that farm. It was a tradition in the family that each generation would add a hectare or two to the farm, so that the next generation would have a little more. Ivan was quite proud that there were now 18 hectares (45 acres)—modest by American standards, but quite substantial by Tovarnik's.

Tovarnik was a small town of some 4,000 people, of which 3,300 were Croatians. The rest were a mix of old and new Serbs. The old Serbs, Ivan explained, had also been on their farms for many generations. As neighbors they got along fine. But new Serbs had been re-settled on land which had belonged to Germans who had been driven off their farms, when the Communists defeated Germany. These new Serbs had been brought up from Montenegro, and they were a mean-tempered lot, often causing trouble.

On the 20th of September (the same day the reservists arrived in Mostar), the shooting started. Civilian irregulars had come into the little town from Serbia and started shooting at the police who fired back. Then the army and reservists had arrived. When some Croatians tried to defend their town, the army had answered with artillery. None of Ivan's family were involved; they all went down in the cellar, where they waited and listened to the shelling.

After three days, some soldiers came to the house, found them in the cellar, and ordered them out. Ivan's son, Drago, nice-looking fellow in his mid-twenties, was the last to come out. One soldier threw him on the ground and started shooting at him. He could feel one bullet hit the ground next to his arm. Then their baby girl started crying, and another soldier pushed the shooter's rifle up in the air—and saved his life.

Why were they shooting at him? He didn't know; probably because he was young, and most of the young men his age had been involved in defending the town.

They put the family in the back of a truck and transported them across the border into Serbia, to the larger city of Sid. There they told the women and the baby girl to go to the Red Cross; they would find accommodations for them. But Ivan and his son were taken to their police station for interrogation.

Drago told what happened to him: "I was taken to a room, where there were about a dozen reservists. Over and over they called me Ustase, and started beating me, kicking me, hitting me with police clubs in the kidney."

But the Ustase were nearly 50 years ago, exclaimed the editor. If any were still alive, they would be old men by now! Surely—"To them, every Croat is an Ustasa!" Drago cried. "Especially if they resist! If you just admit to being

Croatian, you are Ustase! Only if you say you are Yugoslavian, do they not say that. Because only a Serbian would call himself Yugoslavian."

Ivan was returned to his wife, and they were taken back to Tovarnik, where they were returned to their farm. The farmhouse had been slightly damaged by the shelling; they were told to fix it up, paint it, make it like new. All the houses which had not been too severely damaged were now being repaired by their owners.

Three weeks later, the soldiers returned to Tovarnik and ordered all Croatians to leave at once. Don't take anything with them, just leave. And if they refused? They would be shot.

Except for two or three old women, all the Croatians were evacuated. Ivan and his wife were taken back to Split, and dumped at the Red Cross, who eventually were able to re-unite them with the rest of their family. What happened to their farm? They learned later that the next day the army had brought Serb families in and given them the vacated farmhouses, saying "Take them and live in them; they are yours now."

Meanwhile, what had happened to Drago? They had taken him to the prison in Mirkovici, one which had a terrible reputation in old Yugoslavia. He was kept there for a week, and one day he was taken into a room where there was a woman journalist, surrounded by reservists. She asked his name and where he lived and how old he was, and was he married, and she took notes as he answered. Then she photographed him.

After a week, he was taken back to Tovarnik, to stand trial. "Only it wasn't a trial; they just started beating me again. Only this time they were also asking questions. They said they had information which they knew I knew, and

I had better start talking!"

But in the room was a villager, an old Serb, who now spoke up for Drago. He told the reservists that he had had nothing to do with the defense of the town, or with the resistance. So they stopped beating him, and the next day took him back to Sid and gave him to the Red Cross. A week later, his parents arrived, and they were all together again.

How had they come to Mostar? They remained in Sid for three weeks; it took that long for Drago's broken ribs and wounds to heal enough so that he could travel. While he was recovering, a Belgrade newspaper, *Express Politica*, published a story about him, with his picture. It said Drago had butchered Serbs. How could they say that? They needed propaganda, explained Jozo with a shrug, any propaganda. Necessity had been the mother of invention.

What would they do now? Drago looked at his father, who slowly shook his head. Then he went over to the window and stared out.

14

Speak No Evil

The sun was out that afternoon, enhancing the beauty and old-world charm of Mostar. The poplars that lined her streets had lost their leaves, but the shops were bustling, and with no benzine, so were the sidewalks. The trees, the red-tiled roofs, the strolling couples in the winter sun— Mostar was an Impressionist painting that afternoon, and it was easy to see why its inhabitants loved it.

Only one discordant element marred the canvas: the presence of brown-uniformed reservists. In twos and threes, they seemed to be everywhere, browsing, drifting, killing time. Some were drunk, most were sullen. "Our protectors," Jozo muttered, as an army transport full of reservists passed, "our guardian angels."

Suddenly December in Mostar was reminiscent of April in Paris—1940.

That evening, Tuesday, Jozo and the editor met with the European Community Monitoring Team assigned to Mostar. They were staying in the Hotel Ruja, and the meeting took place after dinner, in a nearby cafe. They were eight men in their thirties—from Canada, Holland, Germany, Denmark, and France. Most were in the military or diplomatic services of their respective countries, and all had been asked by their governments to participate. It was a strictly voluntary assignment, lasting on average about three months. Why Canada? Because Canada, along with Poland, Sweden, and Czechoslovakia, had been an invited observer at the European Community conference at which the concept of offering a monitoring effort to Yugoslavia had first been proposed.

What was their mission? The leader of this team was a lieutenant in the Canadian Forces, stationed in Ottawa; he did most of the talking. "Our mandate states: we are here to monitor the situation inside Bosnia-Hercegovina, and to ensure that conflicts or tensions can either be avoided or resolved."

How successful had they been? "It's difficult to gauge. In many cases dialogue continues without our presence."

Was the situation growing more sensitive, more volatile? Or was it calming down? "I think the only safe thing to say would be that the situation changes daily."

It was soon apparent that he was not about to say anything unsafe that evening. The editor shifted the conversation to hockey. Their spokesman was originally from Edmonton; how did he feel about the performance of the Oilers without Gretsky? He was disappointed, he said smiling; he did not want to admit that it could have made such a difference, but it did.

In a little while, the editor tried again. What exactly did the monitoring team do? "A wide variety of tasks. For example, we meet with local military, civilian, and religious leaders, to discuss what the situation is like. In many cases, we go and obtain facts, escort refugee convoys, promote dialogue, and simply monitor."

How far did their jurisdiction extend? "This group goes down to the coast, within Bosnia-Hercegovina, up to Zenica, and north to about sixty kilometers from Sarajevo." How many E.C. monitors were there, all told? About 300; there were other teams in Bosnia-Hercegovina—in Banja Luka and Sarajevo, as well as in the different capitals—Zagreb, Belgrade, and Ljubljana. The one based in Split was now down the coast, monitoring Dubrovnik.

How successful were they at the task of arranging dialogue? "Pretty successful. It depends on whether the parties want to talk or not. Because we cannot make them talk; we can only assist in arranging a dialogue." Any specific examples? "Oh, there are many examples, in every regional center. We've been present in some cases, where negotiations were already going on, or we may have assisted in setting up the meeting, or we provided our services in one form or another, perhaps even in terms of communications to establish contact between the parties. So we have examples in pretty well every location."

Did all sides equally appreciate their presence? At that, the group burst into laughter, but when the lieutenant answered, he was careful to remain impartial: "We continue to negotiate with all parties. . . I suppose that would be a sign of success: we're still communicating."

The editor did not mention the mayor's frustration, or the fact that the Provincial, the head of all Franciscans in Hercegovina, had never been approached by the E.C. team. Instead, he asked what was likely to happen to Bosnia-Hercegovina, if it was to vote for independence? "I cannot answer that question." He looked around the group. "And for any of us to attempt to answer, would be just speculation on each of our parts. We try to stay away from speculation, since it does not provide any useful function."

The editor put his tape recorder away and asked the Frenchman if he thought Fignon would ride in next year's Tour. *"Mais d'accord!"* he quickly replied, *"et Lemond?"* Everyone visibly relaxed.

More time passed, and the recorder came out again. Were there any post-combat areas where they had requested to go, but were told it would be unsafe for them to do so? "Yes," the lieutenant agreed, "there are areas that fall into that category, exactly," but he failed to offer any examples.

The next question was lighter: did they, too, depend on the BBC World Service for their news of what was really going on? "No!" exclaimed the Canadian, "CBC!" "Radio Denmar!" interjected the Dane. "Deutsche Radio!" exclaimed the German. Everyone laughed.

The tape recorder went away again, in the hope of encouraging candor on the final question: During a cease-fire, their primary responsibility was to monitor which side kept it, and which didn't—was that true? Yes. Which side usually broke it? The lieutenant looked at the editor, then said that was confidential information which went in their reports to their superiors in Zagreb. It would be inappropriate for any E.C. monitoring team member—and he looked around the table at each of the others—to offer such an opinion.

The editor thanked him, and as he had requested the meeting, tried to pay the bill. He was graciously told that he could not. But as he was leaving, the Dutch member murmured in an aside to him: When the E.C. monitors first arrived, everyone had said, now with Europe watching, all our problems are over! But they weren't. Now everyone was saying the same thing about the blue helmets. But they would not be able to solve them, either.

Shaking hands with the Canadian, the editor thanked him for his hospitality and complimented him on his professionalism. The Canadian smiled. "Some day, when I am visiting friends in Boston, I will tell you what I think, as a private citizen."

Later that evening, at the monastery where he would spend the night, the editor went back over the interview. He was disappointed—until he realized that the Canadian was only doing his job, and doing it very well.

It was an extremely difficult assignment, because they could hardly refuse to speak to the media. Yet the slightest slip—one ill-advised opinion or injudicious leak—at their level, which later wound up spread across a major newspaper, could jeopardize the entire E.C. mission.

The more he thought about, the more he realized how difficult their assignment was, in personal terms. These were all decent men from democratic societies, in the service of countries whose principles they believed in so deeply that they had dedicated their lives to serving them. They *had* to have profound inner reactions. . . .

What the Dutchman had said stuck with him: The E.C. monitoring teams and the blue-helmeted peace-keepers (if they ever came)—these were the best solutions the world had to offer. And they were not enough.

There was a poignant footnote: On January 18th, three days after the European Community recognized the independence of Slovenia and Croatia, the BBC World Service reported that an E.C. monitoring team, under assurance of anonymity, had confronted the leadership of the federal army in Belgrade with eyewitness accounts of atrocities and video documentation. If these accounts were true, they said, then the officers in charge of those operations were guilty of war crimes.

In the past, Belgrade's customary response to such allegations was to ignore them if possible, or vehemently deny them—and then issue a barrage of identical counter-claims. But this was different; this was an E.C. monitoring team. (One can only conjecture at the drama which must have gone on within the E.C. mission, as they came to agreement on this course of action—if, indeed, they did.)

Twelve hours passed, while the army remained silent . . . twenty-four hours . . . thirty-six. Then the army exploded with accusations of their own, denouncing the allegations as propaganda lies, perpetrated by the European Community to justify their recognition of Slovenia and Croatia! The Croatians were committing far worse atrocities! Worse even than their Ustase predecessors! The Croatians were a genocidal race! It was in their genetic structure to commit genocide!

The world listened to the ranting with shock. And the E.C. monitoring team never received a specific answer.

15

A Time of Faith

When one thinks of another who is special to them, one snapshot usually comes to mind as they turn to that person's place in the memory scrapbook. For the editor, Father Tomislav Pervan would always be standing at the door of the Franciscan retreat house on the hilltop at Glavaticevo, high in the mountains above Konjic. He was there last July, before the reservists came, leading a retreat for young men from Hercegovina about to enter training for the priesthood. Down in Mostar, he was vice-provincial for Franciscan friars, but up here he was just Father Tomislav, relaxed, smiling, helping these young man as they faced the most important spiritual decision of their lives. Father Tomislav had followed Father Jozo as pastor of St. James in Medjugorje, and had guided that parish with a calm and steady hand through most of its turbulent apparition years.

The editor's snapshot of Father Svetozar Kraljevic was also from Glavaticevo, of him playing football (soccer) with the young retreatants—and excelling. Father Svet could be profoundly thoughtful, and inspiring, but he was also free to be free in spirit. Now the spiritual director of a convent outside of Mostar, he had written three books on Medjugorje. Like Father Tomislav, the mountain parish remained close to his heart.

The photo of Sister Janja Boras, on the other hand, was of her walking briskly, gaily along a sidewalk in Worcester, Massachusetts, the freezing February wind swirling about her black habit. She was there for the Medjugorje conference, at the invitation of Medjugorje Messengers' Sr. Margaret Catherine Sims. Back in Mostar, she, too, was a vice-provincial now, responsible for all the Franciscan sisters in the region.

At her convent that Wednesday morning, these three had gathered at the request of the editor who was making a video, to consider how the current situation was affecting not only Medjugorje, but all whose lives had touched by the apparitions—and all mankind.

For Father Svet who began, Medjugorje was no longer a geographical locale. It had become a message, a teaching, a sign given to the Church. In the wake of the war, and the 350 churches destroyed, and the half million people left homeless and wandering—the concept of pilgrimage had an entirely different reality in their lives now, than it had even a few months ago.

Sister Janja, in reference to the bombing in Slavonia, added: "Something scares me more than bombing—to be killed is nothing, really; we will all be dead one day—but, did we really answer her call?" From the beginning, the Blessed Mother had specifically and repeatedly asked people to pray for peace. And now. . . "I hate to talk about the secrets, but—I think what we are seeing now, is what the children saw ten and a half years ago, and what they were so hesitant to mention." She paused. "It really makes me think—and pray more."

Father Tomislav smiled. "For my part, I wouldn't see it so black. . . I like to put Medjugorje in Biblical terms, and here, and in Croatia, and in the whole of Yugoslavia, it's a battle between Hell and Heaven, between the Blessed Mother and Her Son, and the Serpent. And it's the Dragon who is dying—absolutely! It may appear black, but it is not so hopeless. There are always signs of hope!" He thought for a moment. "In a Biblical battle between evil and God, there are many, many sacrifices, but in the end, Jesus will win the victory!"

Father Svet pointed out that the war no longer involved just the tiny section of the world known as Croatia; it involved all humanity. Would the world recognize the right of a little neighbor to exist, when evil wanted to deny that right, and erase its existence? There were two Biblical episodes which pertained: the people of Israel pleading with Pharaoh to let them go. And Jesus standing alone before Pilate, awaiting his judgment. The world was now judging whether Croatia should be allowed to exist. But even as it judged, it was being judged. "You who believe that you have the power in your hands. . . it is God who is the judge—and He speaks last."

Father Tomislav again looked on the bright side: in the agony of this conflict, the Croatian people were rediscovering their own Christian roots and history, and were returning to their faith after forty years of Communist atheism. Their lives had been deprived of spiritual renewal; now they were breaking free of secular values and re-experiencing the profound truth of the Gospel that the earliest Christians knew.

Sister Janja saw it as a time of testing—not only for them, but also for those who were watching what was happening. "I live in Mostar, and every night I wake up numerous times, from detonations and guns. . . as I said earlier, I could be dead any minute. I believe in God, that I'm with Him, alive or dead. But what will happen to those in Europe or the Western world who are seeing this, and are doing very little or nothing?"

She re-affirmed that this was a test which they all had to go through. "I hope we will be purified, and that people, or the world, will learn from us. *We* learn—and maybe for that, we should be more grateful to God. And maybe that's why we've been elected, why we've been put in this spot: to witness in this, the end of the 20th century, that there *is* something more, beside this world."

To Father Tomislav, the ordeal was re-focussing each person's values. "What values am I living, truly? Human values? God's values?. . . Daily we are faced with death. There are guns in the streets, there are tanks. . . It's not important how long we live, but the quality of our life. If I live seventy years of empty life, my life is useless. But if I live maybe forty, fifty years filled with quality, with values, with Jesus —okay, then I can go in peace, as He said; I can die any day."

He chuckled, recalling Paul's warning to Timothy: "All who want to live faithfully in Jesus Christ *will be persecuted!*— It's a good lesson for us. Nothing happens occasionally [by chance]; it's all in Providence." And he emphasized what else Paul said: "If God is for us, *nobody* [can prevail against us!]"

Father Svet seemed to have a different view of what might lay ahead, and what he saw weighed heavily on him. In the past, those who had conquered his people had gone to great lengths to defame the Franciscans with the most ludicrous aspersions. Whenever the enemy panicked, he could be counted on to overplay his hand. And such wild defamation came out of more than mere hatred; it came from fear—that in their martyrdom, they might yet triumph. Like Christ.

"Do not be surprised," he said sadly, "that together with the news of our death, and the destruction of children and homes and churches in this region, also news of our evil doings comes to you. Because this accusation will come together with our destruction, if that is allowed by God. . . I hope that one day, if not while we are here, then in heaven, the truth will be known."

But then his natural buoyancy re-surfaced: "This is a time of faith! That is so true that actually I would rather call it a time of grace. Because it takes away everything that one could, in his confusion, think is important. And now you have nothing to hang onto, nothing to grab, nothing to hope for, but your faith.

"When you see your friends, somehow removed and far away, or when you see many other things taken away, you see this immediate threat upon you, upon your people, upon your church. Then, it is really this grace which tells you: Choose this or that; you don't have many choices left. And to make sense out of all this, you come to God, and God will rescue you. So we see many people now, who have begun praying. There are stories of people who never believed in God, never went to church, never prayed, never received the Sacraments. And as they were staying in their prison cells, beaten up and everything—there was nothing else left *but* to pray!" He paused. "There is a God there—my only hope, my only trust."

Father Tomislav nodded. "As I said before, it is a Biblical

time—where people are forced from their homes, as refugees. They have only a small bag in their hand and the rosary—that's all they have left. Those people are for me the saints of today."

He looked at Father Svet, who added, "For years we have had pilgrims in Medjugorje, coming from all over the world. And there was in this a tiny touch of pilgrimage, where a person for ten days leaves home and is deprived of everything that the home environment gives. Which is a pilgrimage—a taste of the life of Jesus, where the Son of God had no stone to lay His head upon. . ." He smiled. "To be on a pilgrimage is the most profound Christian experience, the basic experience of Christian living. You are actually freed for the moment, to come before the mirror, to see yourself, your own calling. . ."

Slowly he shook his head. "Suddenly we have five hundred thousand people—pilgrims—their homes destroyed, many left without the members of their family. Their whole cities and towns and churches destroyed: they are nothing but pilgrims. So, again, this is a time of tragedy, but ultimately this is a time of grace, where we are learning the way of the Church—the way of Jesus."

And that seemed to say it all.

16

The Cold Places

Wednesday was as cold and bright as the day before, and that afternoon, Father Svet and his editor climbed Podbrdo. The sun was lower now, and it was even colder, but the wind had lessened. Still in a pensive mood from having seen reservists now so close to Medjugorje on their drive over, the brown-robed priest stood beneath the life-sized wooden crucifix and prayed. They were alone on the mountain. A year ago, despite the chill air, there would have been at least a dozen people milling about or praying; now there was no one. The open, rocky place with all the little crosses left by pilgrim groups seemed barren and desolate. Stubs of candles still clung to the boulders around the base of the cross.

With a sigh, Father Svet sat down at the foot of the crucifix and tried to put into words what he was feeling. "It's cold here," he said slowly. "And this is my country. These rocks. . ." he looked at the blackened stones where pilgrims had burned candles or consigned intentions to flame. "The land seems to be burning, and the Cross is above us. This is the land of Croatia." He looked up at the body of Christ hanging on the Cross. "This is the way you see it now. And this is the way it will stand for some time." He looked around him at the open, empty space. "So I find this a very proper place to share some of my concerns and reflections."

On the way up his friend had asked him if he was able to forgive the attackers. He answered that now. "I will speak for myself and for the Church of Croatia: Do we forgive them? Do we pray for them? Do we love them?" He paused, searching the precise words. "The feelings are very difficult to explain and describe, but at this sacred place—which I find is my home—I must say this: Let it be to me—let it be to my land and my people—everything that I wish might happen to them."

He looked out over the valley of Medjugorje, an oasis of peace in a desert of fiery conflict—"I wish them peace. Because I realize that the people of the Croatian nation will never have their own peace, without peace for their neighbor. So, as I'm praying for peace here, I pray for peace which needs to happen to my neighbor." He smiled. "Actually, the peace of my people will only come when it comes to them, so it's impossible to pray for ourselves and not to pray for them."

Thinking of the war and the enemy, he said, "The way they appear now is like fire—burning everything, bringing everything to destruction. . ." His gaze went to the little crosses. "While the fire is around, we'll come to the places like this, and we'll stand here. These are cold places, lonely places."

He looked up at the form on the Cross. "This place is similar to the place Jesus came to, when He was about to come to the end of His life with the Apostles. Every prayer that Jesus said Himself, this land and these people offer now."

He fell silent, and his friend was about to turn off the camera, when Father Svet raised his eyes. "There is something I am even afraid to say." He hesitated. "I don't know what will be the outcome of the next days, the next months. . . One would like to shorten that journey." He paused, thinking again, perhaps, of Jesus at Gethsemane. *Father, if this cup might pass my lips. . .* Then, with a sigh, he said, "Who knows, we may be called to go the whole length of it."

His friend's finger again moved to the camera-switch, but there was one last thought: "If you ever hear a disturbing word from here, you pray. But also do believe that here we are at peace, and we have nothing but peace. And we pray that God may give us that peace which Jesus paid so dearly for us to have."

As they picked their way down the mountain, Father Svet asked his friend: "If you were me, and the war came right here—would you stay? Or would you leave?"

"Happily that won't be your decision," his friend laughed, trying to make light of it. "Your Provincial will decide for you."

But Father Svet did not smile. "There is a tradition among us Franciscans: When it comes to that, each man must make his own decision."

His friend's smile vanished, replaced by tears: "Then you will stay. Refugees will come here, fleeing the soldiers, and you will be caring for them. And you will not leave them."

"Absolutely!" exclaimed Father Svet with a grin.

17

"I am not afraid"

When they reached the rectory, they learned that Vicka was there. Moreover, she agreed to an interview, as soon as she was free. In the meantime, Father Svet introduced his friend to Vitomir Mosa, pastor of the church in Slano. The editor knew the tiny town—a lovely old resort on the Adriatic, about half an hour north of Dubrovnik. He had passed it often, driving to and from Medjugorje.

On October 3rd, the federal army, advancing down the coast towards Dubrovnik, arrived at Slano. There was no military installation there; it had no strategic value whatever. But it was Croatian, and it had a church. As it happened, it was a very old church—five hundred and seventy-one years old. And next to it, the Franciscan monastery of St. Jerome was even older, built in 1399. Together they were a cultural monument, containing priceless works of Renaissance art. The cross was from the fifteenth century, the oil painting of the Blessed Mother had been done in the sixteenth century, as were the paintings of St.

Anthony and St. Jerome, the patron saint of the parish.

It was the Feast Day of St. Francis, when the first planes came over and released their bombs. Expecting the next wave of bombers to target the church, the pastor hurried his little flock out of the church and to a private home. That evening, he led the Mass in the basement of that home, and they prayed the Rosary of St. Francis.

Suddenly there was a tremendous explosion, and the lights went out. Another explosion followed, and another, all night long. After a long time, the pastor ventured a look outside—and saw all Slano in flames.

"Everything was on fire—the homes, the woods around them, everything. It was the most terrible sight one could imagine. In the basement, children were crying without knowing why. Their mothers and the other women were crying, too, but they knew why: their husbands and sons were trying to protect their town, their homes."

They spent that night in the basement, in fear and prayer. In the morning, when the bombing and the shelling ceased, Slano was no more. The army came and told them to leave immediately. But where? How? The army didn't care; just leave!

In the end, they went to Humac, the parish not far from Medjugorje where Father Svet had first been assigned. The pastor kept his flock together. Before he left the church, he had been able to hide the church's records, and take the chalices. But everything else was left behind. They stayed in Humac for two months, living with families of that parish, and then they went to Croatia.

Though Father Mosa was here in Hercegovina, he stayed in touch with his flock, going to them to perform a wedding, a baptism. He celebrated Mass there last Sunday, and was going again next Sunday, because they had to plan how they would celebrate Christmas.

What were the thoughts that stayed with him? The few old women who would not leave and who were killed, had died without a priest. . . the men who were now prisoners of war. . . the old man who was killed in front of his ambulance, and whose body was dumped in the kindergarten. "Every time I see on the television news, mothers crying for their children, I think of Slano," he concluded, his voice breaking.

Vicka looked great. She had put on a bit of weight which suited her, and she seemed considerably less drawn and fatigued than three years before. Her spirit was ebullient. Father Svet agreed to interpret for her and introduced her to the camera. "This face," he smiled, "is known to everyone!" Then realizing who the camera was pointing at, he hastily added, "I mean *this* face: Vicka."

What were her thoughts about Medjugorje these days? "Every time, when I see refugees coming, spending time here, and walking around this little town, my thoughts come like: Why did this have to happen? They had homes, like all of us here. And suddenly they have nothing. And then I say: 'God, You know exactly why.' "

As usual, the words tumbled out, with Father Svet hard pressed to find pauses in which to insert the interpretation. "And this prayer is a real consolation to me, because once I'm able to say it, I know I can give them into the hands of God. And then I am able to say to them: 'If your homes are destroyed, but that is as far as it goes, then more cannot be destroyed.' Then I tell them: 'You see, you lose the home—this little home or large home—you lose it, and you are without it. But then you realize that this' " and she indicated her body, " 'what is in you, is the home of God! And that is something, like your faith, which cannot be destroyed!' "

How did she herself regard this time? "This is a time of grace for all of us, for everyone to think what were the things omitted in the course of our lives. How many times had Our Lady said: 'Pray, pray for peace!' And we asked: why did she ask that? Why did she ask that, if everything was peaceful and nice? But now we realize Our Lady did not speak without a reason. Now we realize why she asked so often."

Pray for peace—could she speak of that peace? "Above all, most important is the peace that the person has in his heart—peace in our family, peace in our community, peace in the surroundings where we are. And with this peace which you have in your heart, is the peace that you could pray with and reach out to others and pray for peace in the world; otherwise, it's only words."

Her thoughts turned again to the refugees. "These people who lose their homes—if they have this inner peace, they will be able to handle their tragic moments much easier. . . and they will believe that there will come a time of their own revival."

What were her own thoughts, with the enemy so near? "My thoughts are that I would never move a step out of my home. I will stay here. I feel now, it's the most important and most valuable thing that I could do: to be here with my people. And I'm not afraid. My feeling is, if the war is to begin, I would be willing to help in any way I can, with any aid to those in need."

How did she feel about those who were threatening them? "My feelings are of pity for them. They have no faith, and no feelings for others. Every time when I pray, I pray for them that God may give light to their hearts and minds, to realize that this leads nowhere. Many are willing to condemn them, but they are not to be condemned; they just don't know. If they did know, they would never come. So, our curse should not be upon them; that would lead nowhere. We really need to pray that God Himself may lead them and show them the way."

Any word for her friends in America? "Greetings to all! I will recommend them to Our Lady, and will keep them in my prayers. And please: you also remember us here in these difficult times, so that God may give strength to everyone to endure."

What sort of thing did she say to her own friends? "I say again and again to the people that I know: Please don't watch TV that much, don't listen to the radio that much. Because in listening to the news on the radio and watching it on TV, we bring this war into our hearts and our souls and our minds. It's better to spend that time in prayer. Otherwise, you burden yourselves and accomplish nothing. You will not help anyone."

She laughed. "I go to bed in peace, because I feel that I have done everything, and the rest I leave in the hands of God."

Father Svet joined her laughter: "And that is the same that I do! I say: I know, God, You have many problems, but I am going to bed."

18

"The Croatian people forgive"

The last person to be interviewed that Wednesday afternoon was Father Slavko Barbaric. Paraclete Press had just published the English edition of *Give Me Your Wounded Heart,* the sequel to his *Pray With the Heart.* Father Slavko continued to be the spiritual director of the visionaries, and long-time friends of Medjugorje agreed: no one had been more changed by the events of the past ten years than he. A scholar who was fluent in four languages (now five, counting English), he had grown more gentle and patient—and humble—with each passing year.

What did he think of the current situation? "For me this situation is like a new argument for the authenticity of the apparitions of Our Lady. Ten years ago, on June 26, 1981, Marija Pavlovic saw her crying and repeating the words: 'Peace, peace, be reconciled,' and 'Pray and fast, because with prayer and fasting you can stop war and suspend even the laws of nature.' You know, it was too foreign—" he shrugged. "If you remember the situation, back in '81, under the structure of Communism, only one war was possible, between America and Russia, and we didn't anticipate one."

He smiled and shook his head at the recollection. "And she said: 'Pray and fast.' You know, she was not able to tell us more, because she does not speak politically. She speaks on another level, for the ears of one faithful person who believes, really. For one who takes seriously the messages of Our Lady, it was enough to understand: yes, we have to pray, we have to fast, we have to convert."

He smiled. "And now we have this war. For me, it is really a cross for our Croatian people—for us. . . Ten years before, we started to pray, and one of the intentions of Our Lady was to stop the war. No war in the history of the world has been so surrounded by prayers, by sacrifices, by fasting as this war."

He frowned. "This war for me is strange in many ways, on many levels. For example, this frustration: we have prayed ten years for peace here. Now many people, many pilgrims, thanks to God, are praying with us. They are with us, and we are surrounding this bad situation with our prayers and with our fasting. Secondly, for example, you may remember during the War in the Gulf, everywhere in the States, in Europe, there were demonstrations against the war, and against the destruction. But these destructions in Croatia have not provoked demonstrations in the streets; people have not come out. Perhaps some, but not the way they did before."

Did he have a thought why? "Somebody asked me why, and I said, I do not know. But I know something else that I do not want to forget: This war was a provocation for the pilgrims of Medjugorje to pray. I know many thousands of people and many hundreds of prayer groups who were gathering for nine days, for three days, for Masses, for prayer. These are Christian demonstrations in one sense, you know. I said, we are not without support."

Was there anything else that seemed strange? He nodded. "No war has finished fourteen times. An occupying army comes in, and they stay until they are driven out. They don't destroy for the sake of destroying. This is not war; it is vandalism. And hate."

Why was God allowing the war to continue? He thought for a moment. "This time may be—" he stopped and smiled. "This is my prayer, not a prediction; I'm not a prophet, you know—a time of purification for us. For the parish, for this region, for the Croatian people. And also, what is happening to us, the Croatian people, may be for everybody who believes, everybody who accepts Our Lady, His Mother." He smiled again. "It's like an *impulse* to pray, and to take seriously her messages. Because she said, and it was said at Fatima: *Convert,* and it's a condition to avoid the war—and perhaps this is happening now, to us, that you may understand. You have to pray, to convert—to avoid something else which could be much worse. She said, please take the messages with seriousness—not fear— seriousness."

Would he comment on the meaning of peace? "When you pray for peace in Croatia, you pray for peace in the world, and not only to stop the war but to stop the destruction of *life.* A letter has come from the Croatian soldiers in Osijek [where the worst fighting was then taking place]. In this letter, they ask the people, doctors from hospitals, and even our government: Stop the abortion! They said, we are in the war, and some of us will be killed. But more dangerous than all the army, all the soldiers, is the abortion for the Croatian people. We ask you, and we beg you: *Stop!*

And protect life from the beginning to the end. They said, perhaps this has happened—and is happening—that we may understand."

Did Father Slavko believe, then, that we no longer valued life, as we ought? "Destructions—we are used to seeing them, to hearing about them. We do not react. Destructions—through abortions, through alcohol, through drugs. How many thousands of young people every year are the victims of drugs? Who reacts? Nobody. And here we wait for Europe or America to react to four or five thousand of us Croatians being killed. Yet they do not react to save their own young people. Who are we Croatians to them?"

He sighed. "We have to love life, to be able to react. So, from the other side, I am not surprised that Europe is so slow, and America. . . But I hope for—and I ask people to pray and help Our Lady bring us—peace."

Was he able to pray for their oppressors? "Of course! I pray every day for the enemies who are seduced. Because these people *are* seduced—by their own ideas, by wanting power. I pray, and we call people to pray, and forgive." He smiled. "Perhaps in this sense, at this point our deliverance will be the result of a great intercession of Our Lady." He nodded, smiling. "The Croatian people forgive."

19

Caritas

As the two young men in the grey uniforms of the Croatian Police stamped their freezing feet and blew on their bare hands, it was hard not to think of them as older boys, playing at being soldiers. They were standing by a corrugated metal shed, in front of which a feeble fire smoldered. The car which had just stopped at this checkpoint high on the side of a mountain, may have been the first they had seen in an hour.

Father Svet's cousin, Jozo Kraljevic, was the driver, and he offered a cigarette to the taller lad, who gratefully inserted it beneath a thin scraggly moustache. The editor unlimbered his videocamera and filmed the mountains they were passing through, more raw and rugged than elsewhere, only partially covered by thin patches of pine, and with no patches of civilization to soften them. A ground mist lingered between the peaks, and anchoring the eastern horizon was the looming presence of snow-capped Mt. Velez.

The trip from Medjugorje to Split would take a little over two hours. Its purpose was three-fold: a half-day, one-on-one crash course in Croatian history, courtesy of Doctor Professor Slavko Kovacic, lecturer in Church History at the College of Theology in Split; a visit to the Church's main refugee relief center; and interviews with the Archbishops of Split, new and recently retired.

The road was more primitive than the main highway down the Neretva Valley to Dubrovnik, and, as it abruptly descended to the Adriatic, more precipitous. But the water was as startlingly blue as before, and the cedars as tall and stark against the azure sky. Split was a modern industrial port with a population of 300,000 (about three times the size of Mostar). As they entered its outskirts, they passed bank upon bank of new apartment buildings. Unlike Mostar, there was no sign of military presence here, although the tall plate glass windows of the new diocesan building next to the cathedral were criss-crossed with strips of tape. While the federal army and navy had been driven far off, there was still the possibility of an air raid. In that event, the cathedral would be a primary objective.

There had been a considerable military presence here two months before. After the navy had blockaded and bombarded Dubrovnik, its gunboats had steamed up the coast to do the same to Split. But unlike Dubrovnik, the city fathers of Split had anticipated this possibility and made preparations. The National Guard had positioned units equipped with captured heavy weapons to guard the approaches to the city, and they even had some captured missiles with which to deal with gunboats.

When they arrived and started firing on the city, to their surprise the city started firing back. To their shock, two of the gunboats were hit. From the bridge, they rang All

Astern Full and got out of range in a hurry—way out of range. Clear over the horizon, in fact.

What they exhibited was the classic behavior of the schoolyard bully. A bully derives his pleasure from inflicting pain on those weaker than himself. He enjoys their fear, as the intimidation process begins, and will prolong it, if time permits. But a bully is also a coward. Confronted with an adversary as strong as himself, and the likelihood of becoming the inflictee, he will turn tail and run.

Dubrovnik, explained Jozo, had so convinced itself that it would never come under attack, that it had made no preparation whatever. Napoleon had left it alone. The Turks had left it alone. Even Hitler, the Attila of the Twentieth Century, had left it alone. No harm would come to the crown jewel of the Adriatic, beloved by the Western world, home of the Dubrovnik Festival of the Arts which was a highlight of the international cultural season. In fact, even to suggest that perhaps they ought to take even minimal precautions, had been looked upon as a breach of faith.

Probably at the heart of their momentous miscalculation was their assumption that the Serbian Communist leadership were men of culture, like themselves. Barely a tenth the size of Split, Dubrovnik had no garrison, no strategic value or importance. Nor was it a refugee center, which might have drawn a lusting foe. It was not even particularly religious. Being of no consequence geo-politically, it would be of no interest to reasonable men.

But reasonable had never been an adjective to describe the current conquest. Hatred, greed, revenge, and sheer vindictiveness were its principle characteristics. Nor could its leaders be accused of appreciating culture; they had deliberately, systematically destroyed every cultural monument they had encountered—which in itself should have been a clue for Dubrovnik, to what might lay in store. And then there was envy: Serbia had no international jet-set attraction to rival Dubrovnik; in fact, they had precious little to attract tourists of any sort.

Why wage war on cultural monuments? Because each monument was immutable proof that Croatian civilization had once flourished there. If you were claiming that that territory belonged in Greater Serbia, because it had once been Serbian, you had better erase all evidence to the contrary, even priceless, irreplacable works of antiquity. The saying that history was written by the victors was taking on a grim new dimension.

Jozo had accompanied the E.C. monitoring team which had met with the army commander, overseeing the assault on Dubrovnik. When asked what had been the purpose of the assault, this colonel replied: to subdue the resistance they had encountered. What resistance? The Croatian police had resisted. Later, a junior officer would confide with satisfaction, that although they might one day be forced to leave Dubrovnik, at least the Croatians would never again enjoy the income that had once come from there.

At the diocesan center in the middle of town, Father Luka was waiting for us. A handsome priest in his 30's with greying hair, he was a man of action. In addition to teaching history and geography, he was a chaplain in the Croatian National Guard. But his main responsibility was to administer Caritas (the Latin word for Charity) which was the name for the Church's relief effort (and which bears no connection whatever with the Birmingham, Alabama organization of that name). In Split, Caritas was actually responsible for far more than just settling and feeding refugees. When Communism ended, the Church was allowed to do openly the sort of charity and social work it had been doing under the table all along. With the government's blessing, they also cared for retarded children, the invalided, the crippled, and nursed the sick, at home and in hospitals.

How many refugees had they processed here in Split? So far, around 18,000. Where had they put them? About 10,000 they had been able to settle in private homes— the rest, in hotels. Was the rate of refugees increasing? Yes, they were now receiving between two and three hundred a day. Where were they mostly coming from? Dubrovnik, but also from Vukovar and Osijek. Other than Caritas, who performed this function? Only the Red Cross, but their only offices were in Belgrade.

He took his visitors to the two little offices which did all the work, and introduced them to two young staff volunteers who took down information from the refugees and entered it into their computer. Both were students at the university—at least, nominally; in actuality, they spent ten or twelve hours a day, right here. The first, Natasha, was twenty and had lived in Vukovar with her mother before they had come here, with her grandparents, to live with her uncle. She had been a student at the university in Osijek, and had transferred here.

Her mother had been a doctor in the hospital in Vukovar, where she remained until the last possible moment, attending the wounded in the basement, since the hospital was a favorite target of the Communist gunners. Ironically, two days before, her mother had been received by President Tudjman who had commended her courage and her willingness to care equally for Serbian and Croatian alike.

The other girl was named Drinka. She was twenty, in her last year of studying economics; in fact, she had only her thesis to finish, to receive her degree and become an economist. But then the war broke out, and—she laughed; she spent her days here, instead of in the library.

Father Luka added that a number of other young volunteers came to prepare packages for the refugee families, sometimes working all night, so that they will be ready for him to deliver in the daytime. What kind of help from abroad did they need most? Everything! [Anyone wishing to help, should contact their local Medjugorje center.]

Archbishop Ante Juric, who had recently assumed the leadership of the archdiocese upon the retirement of Archbishop Franic, was a warrior prince of the Church. Tall, thin, hollow-cheeked and hollow-eyed, he was reminiscent of an age when the Pope led troops into battle.

"Our biggest problem in Croatia is refugees," he declared. "You can imagine how terrible it is—550,000 banished from their homes, exiled. Leaving behind everything. And when the invader is driven out, they have nothing to return to. Because when they leave, the enemy loots and plunders their homes, taking everything, and then burning the house down. You have seen the pictures on television, villages leveled to the ground, nothing left standing. They make certain that the exiles have nothing to come home to."

What explanation did the army give? "No explanation! But their plan is clear: The Serbs want to erase the Croatian people from the provinces, in order to annex them into Serbia. In Slavonia, there are five times as many Croatians as Serbs. But they want Slavonia. In Vukovar itself, there were twice as many Croatians as Serbs."

And their plan? "To create Greater Serbia! They have

this peculiar assertion: wherever there is even one Serb, that is Serbia." He smiled, without humor. "So you Americans should be worried, because you must have a few Serbs living there." The smile vanished. "But this is the logic they follow, as they conquer and destroy Croatian territory."

How did he feel about the E.C.'s efforts to achieve peace? "It is difficult for us to understand the hard-hearted impartiality of western politicians, when they treat us as equally to blame for this war. One is plainly the victim and one the aggressor, yet," he shook his head, "they put us in the same bag!"

Months of frustration had built up behind his outburst. "Fourteen times they have signed cease-fire agreements, each time knowing that they were going to break them! The European monitors could tell you, if they chose. They could tell you that our soldiers do not take civilian prisoners. Theirs do. And our prisoners are well-treated. But theirs— you ought to see the difference, when prisoners are exchanged!"

Why was that? "Because we are Christians! We are sinners, of course, but our faith does not permit us to behave in certain ways."

But were they not Christians, too? "Only a third of them are baptized, and for most, it's only nominal. Their faith does not seem to be that important to them."

That seemed like a rather blanket statement; did he— "Do you know what they tell their soldiers? If they surrender or are captured, we will torture them!"

Did he know that for certain? "In Vukovar, a Serbian sergeant was wounded, and as our guardists approached him, he cried out, 'Kill me! Do not torture me!' The guardists didn't know what he was talking about. They carried him to the field hospital, where he was treated the same as the wounded Croatian soldiers on either side of him. That was when he told them, what all of them had been told over and over again. And later he bore witness to it, on television." The archbishop paused. "For years the Serbs have been lied to and filled with hatred against the Croatians. That hatred has come to a peak now and produced this war."

Now he had a question for the interviewer: "I am puzzled by the silence of your president. America was once the champion of democracy. Well, we are a democracy, overrun by a Communist aggressor who wants to destroy a people, wipe out their culture, and absorb their homeland into his state—how can he stand aside, passive? Does our suffering not mean anything to him?"

The editor shook his head, unable to offer any explanation.

"The Holy Father has not stood aside," exclaimed Archbishop Juric, referring to his own commander-in-chief. "He has supported Croatia in her struggle to survive. Do you know that our guardists go into battle with rosaries around their necks? That is unique in all history. It is also inspired, because this is not a normal war; it is a spiritual war, between God and Satan.

"This is not the first time that we have been on the frontier of a conflict between godlessness and Christianity. For three centuries we were the bulwark of Christianity, that held back the Ottoman Empire from spreading over Europe. How much it has cost us as a nation, you can understand, if you consider that at the time of our King Tomislav [tenth century], the number of Croatians was equal to the number of English. Today in our homeland there are four and a half million Croatians, and in England there are 65 million. It is not because we have lived less modernly. It is because we have been constantly killed during the centuries. Europe seems to have forgotten this."

To return to the spiritual, what difference had prayer made? "I must say that I am convinced that the fact that we still exist, that we have not been completely crushed by the army, is only thanks to the mercy of Heaven—asked for and gotten by prayer, both here and in the whole world. The Holy Father called upon the whole world to pray for Croatia, and that prayer is our strength. It is our hope. Not politicians. How else to explain how we could, empty-handed, have resisted for months such a huge army?" He smiled, with humor. "So actually these are the signs of Heaven. You can almost feel them with your fingers, physically!" The smile grew warmer. "And these are signs of God's love for us! As the Scriptures have indicated, something truly Messianic is happening here!"

By contrast, his predecessor, Archbishop Franic, was a gentle soul, tucked away in his little apartment. He was a short, heavy-set man in his early 70's, whose eyes were starting to go—which was a great frustration to him. All his life, he had looked forward to having the time to pursue scholarship, and now that he did, he could barely read the texts he wanted to study. He had taken part in Vatican Council II, and was in the process of preparing his speeches and interventions for publication.

How did he feel about the Croatia's prospects in the immediate future? "What is happening in the former Yugoslavia is what is happening in the former Soviet Union. You have Russia that would like to keep the Ukraine, and

Serbia that would like to keep Croatia. In both places, it is the Communist element which wants to hold on, and the democratic element which wants to be free."

And the E.C.? "They don't understand our situation. Especially Britain and France. They are afraid that Germany is going to gain influence in Slovenia, Croatia, and Bosnia-Hercegovina. And they are more afraid of Germany, than they were of the Soviet Union." His voice grew stronger. "They should be more concerned about Communism gaining back its strength, than about Germany. If Communism succeeds here, it could eventually be great trouble for them." He sighed. "Anyway, it's all in God's hands."

Friends of Medjugorje in America are all extremely grateful for his rebuttal of the Bishop of Mostar—any comment? "Yesterday, a group of Italian intellectuals called on me. Referring to the declaration of our bishops, under the influence of Bishop Zanic, that they would not or could not recognize that Our Lady was there, one of the Italian gentlemen commented: 'Jesus said to the Jews: Woe to you, Jerusalem, because you did not recognize the day of your visitation, when I visited you.' " He shook his head. "After so many so many wonderful healings at Medjugorje, after so many conversions, so many prayers and penances, and after so many prayer groups forming all over the world. . ." He was speechless.

But ironically, by his repeated attacks on the apparitions, may not Bishop Zanic actually have helped Medjugorje? Because of him, rebels and skeptics within the Catholic Church and without were far more open-minded as they approached the phenomenon, than they would have been, had the Church's local authority quickly embraced it.

The old priest was not convinced. "That may be true

from one aspect. But on the other hand, he actually prevented our bishops from seeing, from realizing the truth of what is happening there. He closed their eyes." He looked up, his own eyes immensely sad. "You see, the Jews—they did not recognize Jesus, and they killed Him in the end. I agree that in so doing, they made it easier for the gentile world to recognize Him. But Jerusalem—and Israel, in general, as a whole—were punished for that." He paused and lowering his eyes, murmured: "I'm afraid for my homeland."

That like Israel and the Jews, it would be punished? He nodded. "I'm afraid." Then he brightened. "But still I hope. After all, it is not quite the same. And Zanic and the other bishops do recite the rosary. They love Our Lady, after all!"

20

"She could easily stop that war"

On the second Friday in Advent, St. James Church celebrated the Feast of St. Lucia. The church was decorated for Christmas, and as the Mass began, it was completely full. There was a spirit of quiet joy—in fact, the Spirit of God was so present, that everyone knew it and was smiling. *The light shone forth in the darkness, and the darkness could not overcome it.* . . .

After the Mass, the editor interviewed Marija in Father Slavko's office, where his secretary and assistant, Milona von Hapsburg, acted as interpreter. The two of them shivered in their winter coats, for there was hardly any heat in the building.

In the ten years since the apparitions had begun, the visionaries had grown into young adults now, and two of them were married. But friends of Medjugorje who had voraciously read all the early books and memorized the photographs in them, still tended to think of them as children. They would have been startled to see the poised and charming young woman that Marija had become. But as soon as she spoke (in fluent Italian), they would have been reassured: the deep spirituality was still there. And now, under the warm smile, there was also sadness and compassion.

What did she have to say to those of us who loved Medjugorje? "I would ask you to pray yet more, because it's a moment now when we're very much in need of prayer. I would ask you now in a special way for prayers. Because until now, probably we prayed a lot for others, but now, at this moment, we feel things have changed. . .

"We suffer—and not only ourselves here, but we suffer, united with our people. As it says in the Bible, if one part of the body suffers, then the whole body suffers. And so those people who love Medjugorje, they are part of that suffering as well, united with us. So we would ask for much prayer from their side."

How did she feel about the war that was tearing Croatia apart and threatened to come there? "I feel bad about it. Very often, I feel I could have done more. I could have listened to the messages of Our Lady with more responsibility. I feel, on the other hand, that we need to do more now—not only myself, but all of us who are involved—everybody, of course, in his own way. First of all, with prayer, of course, because prayer is the most important and the richest part. And afterwards, with many little ideas."

She thought a moment, then added gravely: "Also with perhaps the reality, which we speak about freely, and we express it: It's not a war between Croatians and Serbs. It's a war against democracy, the war of Communism. And I believe most of all, it's a war which is not human. Because we can see the reactions in those who kill. They have satanic reactions; they're abnormal."

Had Marija heard anything recently from the Blessed Mother, which she would care to pass along? She nodded with a smile. "Three days ago, Our Lady gave a message; we were with a group that was having a retreat. Our Lady said that she asks for more prayers. Because, she said, she could easily stop that war, if she had more prayers. And so, she asks us to pray yet more."

It was twelve days before Christmas—would she like to send a Christmas greeting to her friends in America? "Yes," she beamed. "I wish you all a Happy Christmas. . ." And then she grew thoughtful. "I also wish for you, that you pray that we could have this Christmas also, as a sign of peace. Because when Jesus was born, Peace was born, in a particular way—peace between man and God."

IV

The Future

21

The War Outlook

Putting through a call to Mostar was enough to try the patience of Job (and getting through to Medjugorje was even worse). What was more, it seemed axiomatic that the more urgent the reason for the call, the less likely the caller was to get through, or to actually reach the person being called. Then, after two hours of trying, the connection might finally be made—only to have an echo or constant fading, and at the crucial moment, a disconnect.

Conversely, when the call was not urgent—really, more of an encouragement than anything else—then as likely as not it would go right through, nema problema. And the person on the other end would sound like he was three blocks away. That was the way it was a few days ago. The call was intended for Father Svet, but he was not at his convent (nor was anyone else who could speak English).

"Father Svet—Mostar?"

"Ja, ja, Mostar."

The subsequent call was clear as a bell and answered

on the first ring, not by Father Svet, but by a familiar voice, nonetheless: Father Tomislav Pervan! Who said that until a moment before, he had not been in the monastery at all.

How were things? "Better." Better than what? "Than when you were here in December."

How were—the editor ran down the list of their friends. Everyone was fine. Was the cease-fire holding? "Some shooting today, outside Zagreb. And Osijek. And Vincovci. But everywhere else, quiet."

How did it look for the blue helmets coming? "Good! Today the president in Belgrade sent an invitation to the Secretary General of the U.N., inviting him to send troops. All parties signed."

That *was* good! Was it still as tense in Mostar? "A little less."

What was the main concern there? "No food. Or medicine." Why? "All the borders are sealed; it is like we are under blockade. And the money is worthless." How many dinars to the dollar? "On the blackmarket, two hundred." *Two hundred!* "That is today; maybe more, tomorrow."

Well, we were all praying for them. "Good! We pray for you, too! Give everyone a hug!" As he hung up, the editor smiled; Father Tomislav did not used to be the hugging type.

In an earlier report, Father Svet had been less optimistic. At the Croatian National Guard checkpoint near Miljkovici, a squad of Serbian irregulars had appeared, disarmed the guardists, and sent them away. It was a clear-cut provocation, calculated to goad a response from the vastly-outnumbered Croatians. But the guardists did not retaliate.

The irregulars had moved their tent encampments close

to the road, warning villagers to stay away from them. Early one morning about a month ago, one poor old woman found out why. She was driving her cow to pasture, as she always had, and noting the new tents nearby, had paid no attention to them. All at once, there was a tremendous explosion directly in front of her; her favorite cow had been blown to smithereens. It had stepped on a newly-planted land mine.

Father Svet learned of this from her neighbor, in the course of making the home-blessing calls that Franciscan priests in Hercegovina traditionally made at the beginning of the New Year. When he asked after the old woman whose home was now empty, her neighbor told her of the cow. While the old woman had not been physically harmed, she was so traumatized that she had packed a bag and left, going to Germany to live with relatives.

As of March 2, the UN-brokered peace was, by and large, still holding. That was one of the two pre-conditions to the arrival of a 14,000-man U.N. peacekeeping force. The other was that both sides should want the force to come.

Theoretically, there was nothing delaying them. Croatia's President, Franjo Tudjman, had compromised his previously adamant insistence that he retain civil control over Serbian enclaves in Croatia, and that part of the U.N. peace-keeping force be stationed along the pre-existing border between Croatia and Serbia (which would have amounted to *de facto* recognition of that border). To have them there would put the world's eyes on what the Serbian Communists had done during their conquest of eastern Croatia—the atrocities, the wanton, senseless destruction, the transplanting of Serbian families into the homes and onto the farms of Croatians. And it would also have curtailed the continuing flow of civilian irregulars from Serbia into

Croatia and Bosnia-Hercegovina. As grating as it must have been to accept the imposition of an external solution in Croatia's internal affairs, it was the only way to get the blue helmets to come. And without them, there would be little chance of ever regaining the territory which the army had taken.

As for Serbia's President, Slobodan Milosevic, he, too, had compromised, though accepting the legitimacy of the right of the U.N. to intervene sounded the death-knell of old Yugoslavia as even a concept. Croatians had ceased using the word Yugoslavia, from the day the Communist system had self-destructed. But old hands in Western diplomatic circles had been exceedingly loathe to let it go, and Milosevic had played to them, casting Serbia and Montenegro in the role of fighting to maintain Yugoslavian stability. But now, even the most reluctant diplomat would have to accept its demise.

As if to mark the transition, the BBC World Service had begun referring to "the former Yugoslavia"—and hypothesizing about a new "rump-state" of Serbia and Montenegro. Milosevic had no choice but to moderate his position and accept the U.N. peace-keeping force, for the increasingly outspoken anti-war sentiment in Serbia was now seriously challenging his leadership. Claiming that his dream of Greater Serbia was ruining the republic, they were demanding his ouster—and there were too many of them to jail them all.

Nevertheless, there were endless procedural delays, and the further the blue helmets were put off, the greater was the danger of the cease-fire collapsing. Under tremendous strain, it was already beginning to fray at the edges; the number of incidents and outbreaks of hostilities was increasing.

If they did not come soon, Bosnia-Hercegovina was doomed. In a national referendum on February 29 and March 1, that republic had voted for independence, and the Serbian minority (about a third of the republic's population) had boycotted the election. As this book went to press, Bosnia-Hercegovina (and Medjugorje) were in greater peril than at any previous time. For Communist Serbia would never simply let it go. It would demand the republic be partitioned, and would attempt to hold onto as much as possible. And Croatians and Serbians had both made it clear that they would prefer to die fighting for their freedom, rather than accept involuntary annexation.

Nor could the federal army afford to simply release Bosnia-Hercegovina, the last solvent republic. For the government in Belgrade, its treasuries exhausted, had done what governments in financial panic always did: it had started printing money. It was the only way they could meet the enormous payroll of all the people in the military and the civil government. But paper money with no backing was just that: paper money. And the people knew it. As their confidence in the currency fell, the government found itself having to print more and more. (With great foresight, they had made certain the mint was in Belgrade, not Zagreb.)

Under Communist Yugoslavia, the rate of exchange had held steady, at around seven dinars to the dollar. Last summer, a month after the beginning of the war, the rate was still fairly steady, though it had jumped to twenty-three dinars to the dollar. Then in September, the Belgrade government printed fifteen billion dinars, and by mid-December, though the rate was still officially pegged at twenty-three to the dollar, on the blackmarket, it was fifty-five in Mostar, seventy in Medjugorje. (The blackmarket was not some shady character in a back alley, whipping open a briefcase; it was wherever payment was accepted in dollars. And with the rate of exchange escalating daily, everyone preferred dollars to dinars.) There must have been another huge press run at the mint recently, for the current going rate to have quadrupled in the past two months.

If you happened to be a totalitarian waiting in the wings, runaway inflation could actually be an asset. For it literally wiped out the middle class—the businessmen, the professionals, the shopkeepers—who would represent the greatest obstacle to your accession. Runaway inflation had been an ambitious Hitler's greatest ally. But if you were already in power, as Milosevic was, it was a disaster. When the people could not afford the cost of bread, sooner or later it could cost you your head.

Not accustomed to placating anyone, let alone play the politician Milosevic was desperately trying to modulate his tone. A major anti-war protest was scheduled in Serbia for March 9. If accompanied by a widespread general strike, it could mean the end of his regime. . . .

Meanwhile, Secretary General Boutros-Ghali was moving swiftly, before the fragile UN-brokered cease-fire collapsed entirely. The force should be in place within two to three weeks after the General Assembly's final approval—and the only thing that could hold that up would be determining who was going to put up the $400 million that it was likely to cost. It was possible that the first contingent of blue helmets could arrive by mid-March.

The great imponderable remained the federal army. With enough food, fuel and munitions to sustain full-scale combat operations for several months, it was answering to no one. But bit by bit, its *raison d'etre* was being chipped away. At its present strength, it was ten to twelve times larger than the defense of any rump-state could justify. Would it idly accept decimation? Or would it find some new reason for its existence? If the anti-war (anti-army) movement in Serbia succeeded in toppling Milosevic, and if Bosnia-Hercegovina threatened to pull away, who would be left to support them?

One indication that the old generals were not about to quietly fade away was that, when they withdrew all combat troops from Croatia, instead of recalling them to Serbia, they had re-routed them into Bosnia-Hercegovina, instead. In fact, practically the entire federal army was now encamped in that republic, waiting. . . .

22

If We Pray. . .

The only thing that has kept all hell from breaking loose until now, has been prayer. That was the one good thing that came out of all the wild rumors of September: for those who cared about Medjugorje, it brought viscerally home just how precarious was the situation of their friends over there—and still is. They are defenseless. Before the world gets done wringing its hands, it could be all over.

It would have been over three months ago, except for one thing: prayer. Enough people prayed. The Blessed Mother's monthly message for November, the shortest ever, consisted of three words: *Pray, pray, pray!*

And we did. We prayed in obedience—even if we had little confidence that our prayers would make any difference.

God honored that obedience, as He always does. Somewhere, in some high army command, a general changed his mind. The plan to provoke and attack was put on hold—for the moment.

In December, the situation was absolutely critical—a tinder-dry forest at the mercy of a careless match. But in January, the picture began to brighten. The UN-brokered cease-fire was holding—when fourteen previous cease-fires had broken down. On both sides, the leaders were compromising —a double miracle. And by mid-February, it had brightened still more—to the point where the war news (or peace news) from Croatia no longer merited newspaper print. In fact, the only way to keep track of what was happening, was by shortwave radio* or the BBC World Service which a number of public radio stations carried (usually an hour or two before dawn).

We had prayed hard for peace—and for the moment, peace seemed to be at hand. Tour agencies were even beginning to plan pilgrimages again.

Prayer had done this—nothing but prayer.

But would we continue to pray?

Medjugorje had been the instrument by which literally millions of hearts had been quickened and drawn to the heart of God. Would these hearts remain warm? Or would they cool and harden?

The prophet Joel, speaking for God, had written: *"And in the latter days I will pour out my spirit upon all flesh. . ."* It was hard not to believe that we were indeed in the latter days—and had been, for some time. In the twentieth century there had been three great outpourings of God's Spirit. The first came at the beginning of the century with the Pentecostal Movement. It reached around the world, awakening men and women to the role and enabling power of the Third Person of the Trinity. But the movement

---

*7315 MHz—Radio Zagreb 7:00-7:15 PM, EST, repeated at Midnight. On Saturdays, 8:00-8:15 PM.

was rejected by the main Body of Christ, and withdrew unto itself. Gradually it calcified and in its own way became as rigidly structured as the mainline denominations from which it felt estranged.

Half a century later, God again poured out His Spirit. This time *all* denominations were affected—so thoroughly that the Body of Christ (with a few fundamental and evangelical exceptions) had to accept it, albeit in some areas with great reluctance. In the beginning, the Charismatic Renewal shone with promise. Catholics and Protestants alike were caught up in the thrill of discovering the supernatural gifts of the Spirit, and the power of prayer. Classic revival, of the sort that had galvanized America in previous centuries, again swept the land. Men and women devoured every book and audio cassette on the Holy Spirit they could get their hands on, and traded them among Charismatic friends. (There were no videotapes in those days.) They thought nothing of driving a hundred miles to hear an anointed speaker, or spending a thousand dollars to fly to a Charismatic conference. They formed prayer groups, prayed for all manner of healings—nothing was too much to ask of God—and rejoiced, as time after time, He answered their prayers.

So what happened? Why had the Charismatic Movement not transformed the Body of Christ? Because, after the initial thrill of embracing the reality of a loving, caring God, not too many were interested in taking the next step. As pleased as God the Father is at the first baby steps His children take, He is not satisfied, until they are walking erect and growing into adulthood, cooperating with His Spirit, as He conforms them ever more to the image of His Son.

The trouble with the Charismatic Movement was that for the most part, it stopped moving. It is painful to grow up. Painful to do as the Baptist did, when he wrote: *I must decrease, that He may increase.* Painful to admit that we are sinners, and are going to go on committing the same sins, until we cooperate with God, as He shows us where He would have us change, and gives us the grace to do so. It is painful to have to keep going back to God, to confess and ask forgiveness again, to accept His forgiveness and the cleansing of His blood again. Not for nothing is it called the Way of the Cross.

Modern Christians don't care for pain. The abounding grace of God is supposed to do away with that. We sing in the Spirit and rise above the pain. We affirm one another and ignore the pain. We grimace when Vicka speaks of suffering as a gift. We discount the examples of all the saints who accepted their suffering and embraced their crosses. "But that was then, and this is now; surely God does not expect *that* of *me*." We do not accept that suffering cannot be avoided in this life, and we can either suffer in Christ, or outside of Him.

Too many of us in the Charismatic Movement did not want to suffer. Since maturing invariably involved pain, we chose to remain in our infancy, where everything was always new and exciting and wonderful. We continued to share our excitement with others, like a tree sending out feeder roots in all directions. But we failed to put down a tap root—the deep root, born of pain, that would keep the tree standing, when the whirlwind came (as it surely would).

But as the Charismatic Movement was meant to grow, when it preferred to stay in the crib, it did not just remain an infant; it became a misshapen dwarf. Things which started out as good things, became perverted. When the Movement shunned the pain of ongoing repentance and forgiveness, it denied itself the one thing which would cleanse and purify it. When self refused the pain that came each time it was stretched out on the Cross and nailed there, it increased as Christ decreased.

Why recall all that here? Because the third (and some say, final) outpouring of His Spirit is in danger of going the same way.

The modern Marian Movement may not have begun with Medjugorje, but Medjugorje has become the prominent jewel in its crown. This in no way diminishes any of the other appearances of the Blessed Mother, past or present; wherever God has sent her, under whatever circumstances, for whatever mission, each is profoundly significant. In the past two decades there have been more than forty different recorded sites of apparitions, widely recognized if not yet approved. And there are undoubtedly many more which are not generally known. They are taking place all over the world, and while some may be fraudulent, it may well be that nearly all of them are authentic. This is her time. It may be the enemy's time, but it is also her time.

For whatever God's reasons, Medjugorje has received the most attention and the most pilgrims. That should not be a cause of jealousy, but it is. It is unfortunate that, when one part of the Body is blessed, all other parts cannot rejoice in the blessing. But it is indicative of the malaise that is endemic today—and why history is in danger of repeating itself.

From the beginning of apparitions at Medjugorje, right up until the war last summer, the response of pilgrims was similar: awe, wonder, great enthusiasm, and a determination to go home and *live* the messages. Many did. In living them, they *became* the message of Medjugorje. Their lives were permanently altered—*converted*—and others were drawn to what had changed them. Their lives, too, were changed. They might never go to Medjugorje, but wherever they were, Medjugorje was there. And their lives touched others, whose lives touched others. . . .

We devoured all the books we could lay our hands on, swapped video and audio cassettes, went to hear the speakers and attend the conferences, joined Mir Groups and Medjugorje Centers, prayed for healings and miracles—nothing was too big for God! In our enthusiasm, we could not wait to tell all our friends about it—forgetting her admonition to first let it become a reality in our lives. God did call some of us to spread the message of Medjugorje by speaking to groups; others of us wanted to so badly, we convinced ourselves that He was calling us, too.

But even as the feeder roots went out, the tap root was not going down—not to the depth that was called for (and would soon be needed).

This was not true of all. For some, the process of conversion, begun in the little mountain village on the other side of the world, never ceased. They accepted the pain that went with the Way of the Cross. *If any man would come after me, let him deny himself and take up his cross daily and follow me.* . . He led them to the Cross, where they discovered it was not a post but a door. They went through the Cross and into the Resurrection Life. For awhile, they were with Him in the heavenlies, but then they came back down to earth. And began the process all over again. Yet each time they went through the pain of the Cross, they left a little more of self behind them.

Compassion, they discovered, was not one of the Gifts of the Spirit which Paul had enumerated to the believers in Corinth. It could not be activated at will. Nor was it one of the Fruits of the Spirit, which he had told the

Galatians about. Compassion was the Wine of the Spirit. And the only way to make wine was by crushing grapes.

There were no shortcuts on the Way of the Cross, no magic prayer or formula that would hasten the journey. But with the inevitable pain and suffering, there was always commensurate grace. And every so often, when the ascending pilgrim became discouraged (not full of self-pity, but in need of encouragement), the Comforter would bring him or her to an open place, where they could catch a glimpse of how far they had come. Then they could go on, with hearts full of gratitude and quiet joy.

And gradually, without their awareness, other hearts would respond to what was happening in their heart. Others would see Jesus in them, and would be drawn to go the same Way, no matter what the cost.

Medjugorje has produced a surprising number of such saints. Some are well-known. Many more will never be well-known. But you know them. They're the ones who make you smile, every time you think of them. The ones you can't wait to be with again. They may be in habits or teaching school, driving trucks or driving kids, working in offices or making homes. You love them, because you love Jesus, and it is so easy to see Him in them. And when you see Him there, you want Him in you, too, the same way.

Such wine may have come from other apparitions; it has definitely come from Medjugorje. That may be why God has seen fit to elevate that place. And possibly that was why the Blessed Mother went there—because she knew that in the soil of that place, the root would go deep.

Unfortunately, for many of us, perhaps millions of us, the deepening process has not continued the way it should have. We came home and did our best to live the messages— for awhile. But eventually the sense of urgency died away.

It no longer seemed a matter of life and death that we hang onto what we had found there, and keep on surrendering more and more of our lives. And forgive and forgive and forgive. And go on and on, facing sin and confessing it and getting reconciled with God and whomever else we needed to.

We got tired of battling self. And stopped. Imperceptibly our hearts grew a little colder and a little harder. Until we had lost that wondrous awe that we had first known, and the willingness that went with it—willingness to do anything He asked, no matter what. And eventually, not even a trip back to Medjugorje could recapture it.

We still thought of ourselves as Medjugorje pilgrims, whose lives had been forever changed by that place. But our lives had not gone on changing. Self had not continued to decrease, that He might increase. More and more, we had reverted to our old natures. And were no longer primarily interested in cooperating with the Holy Spirit, as He sought to conform us to the image of the Son.

Until finally, without our awareness, instead of giving Medjugorje a good name, we were giving it a bad one. "I don't know about those Medjugorje people—they're so impulsive and abrasive. They never seem to think things through, or are the least bit sensitive to the feelings of others. They're self-absorbed and arrogant—and have you noticed how jealous they are of one another? And how unethical? If that's what Medjugorje is all about, you can have it!"

The same things, to the very word, were said of Charismatics a generation ago.

All that can change, right now. The Blessed Mother had pleaded with us to pray for peace. Who in his or her heart can say that they have responded to her appeal, as they knew they ought? Not even Marija—and her whole life is a prayer.

It *must* change, right now. One has only to read the papers or watch the news, to know that the situation over there is at least as grim as it was in November.

If we will pray as we know we should, if we will get back to living the messages, then peace will prevail, and Medjugorje will be spared. Our prayers can buy enough time for world opinion to coalesce, for U.N. resolve to stiffen. Who knows, perhaps even for the United States to become involved.

But if we do not pray. . . .

23

If We Do Not Pray. . .

If we do not pray, all hell *will* break loose. On March 4, according to the BBC, Serbian militants were reportedly converging on Sarajevo, and Muslims were manning barricades against them. Having boycotted the referendum, said the BBC, the militant Serbs wanted to convince the outside world that the situation in Bosnia-Hercegovina was so volatile that it would be best to delay recognition of that republic's independence.

The violence could spread to Mostar in an instant. A fight could break out in a cafe, at a checkpoint a squad of reservists could humiliate a pair of Croatian policemen beyond endurance, a civilian irregular could molest a child in a village. . . .

The pretext is of little consequence; the general staff has already drawn up its battle plan and marching orders. (Whatever its shortcomings, this army is justly renowned for its long-range planning.) The supplies are loaded, the transports are fueled, the officers and non-commissioned officers have been briefed.

The operation will begin at night, so that by dawn many objectives will have already been achieved. For the 2nd Army Corps, the primary objective will be to secure the main highway system linking Sarajevo to the coast. To accomplish this, they will drive northeast up the Neretva River valley, toward Konjic and Sarajevo. At Jablanica, they will divide, sending a force northwest up that tributary towards Bugojno and eventually Banja Luka. Their reserve force, in Mostar and Trebinje, will strengthen its hold on the lower Neretva.

The 2nd Army Corps will not bother with the Croatian towns and villages within reach of Mostar. They will leave Medjugorje—and Citluk and Ljubuski and Miljkovici—to the reservists and the civilian irregulars. Which is fine with the latter; they have been waiting for action ever since September 20th. They would rather be up in the mountains, killing Croatians, than down on the Neretva plains, walking behind tanks.

In that region, the Croatian National Guard will be vastly outnumbered. At best, all they can hope for is a delaying action—hoping to check the advancing enemy long enough to enable the townspeople and villagers to evacuate their homes and get safely away, probably in the direction of Split. They cannot mount a standing defense of each village in the enemy's path; too many men would be lost in hopeless confrontations.

Their overall commander will be under orders to preserve as much of his force as he can, withdrawing before they themselves are killed or captured. In time, they will defend high ground of their own choosing, drawing the enemy further away from their bases, then falling on them in ambush. In the end, they will win—but it will not be in front of Medjugorje.

Like the Franciscans, they will give each man from that area the right to make his own decision. Many will elect to stay and try to defend their homes. And they will be joined by other men from the villages. In fact, all but the oldest and the youngest will go to the barricades.

As the enemy approaches Medjugorje, they must first fight their way through Citluk, and it will be block by block. There will be much shelling; the reservists have howitzers and trucks to pull them, though most of the tanks will be with the 2nd Army Corps, back on the highway system. Citluk will prove far more difficult to reduce than the enemy anticipates. (Just as Vukovar and Dubrovnik, and now Osijek and Vincovci.)

There will be many casualties among the civilian population, and all who are ambulatory will head for Medjugorje—not because there are doctors or medical supplies there, but because they will be hurt and traumatized and desperate to find someone who will care for them. Medjugorje will naturally come to mind, for Medjugorje has been helping the hurt and traumatized for years. Surely there, they will be safe.

"We're going to Medjugorje; where are you going?"

"We have family in Split."

"Too far; you'll never make it. Come with us to Medjugorje. The *Gospa* is still appearing there. (Vicka has said, she will not leave.) We'll be safe there."

But nothing whets the appetite of a pack of wolves like the sight of a wounded prey, hobbling to escape. All those hurt refugees, gathering in the same place. . . .

Casualties and terrified refugees will stream into Medjugorje—and ministering to their needs, comforting the wounded, praying with the dying, will be the priests and sisters of Medjugorje, Father Slavko and Father Svet among them.

Each evening, for the rosary and the Mass, the church will be unable to hold all the people; the outdoor altar behind, and the whole plaza in front, will be thronged. In their worship, God will be right there with them—they will feel His presence. For He loves them—and is preparing them for what is to come. By opening heaven to them in this way, He is making it easier for them to leave earth. Their hearts are already with Him; their souls and spirits will soon be also.

For by now most know in their hearts that they will never leave Medjugorje.

The light that has always come from that place will be stronger now—brighter and more far-reaching than it has ever been. Wave upon wave of blue-white light will emanate from there, out and farther out, to all parts of a darkened world.

The enemy has hated that light, from the moment it began. Some have even speculated that he engineered this conflict as a cover for his attempt to extinguish it. But wherever people pray with the heart, there is light—and for centuries, throughout this tortured land, there have been people leaving little pools of light in secret places where they have prayed. He hates them all.

There is no question that he has harbored a special hatred for the light from this village which has kindled and rekindled so much light elsewhere. And now, it lays within his grasp—meek and helpless, a lamb on his black altar, awaiting the thrust of his upraised dagger.

The sun will rise brightly on the last day. The sky will be clear, the cross on Mt. Krizevac will be shining—a visual prayer, blessing the valley. The bells of St. James will summon people to morning prayer. Goats will bleat and frolic on their way to pasture. The roosters have long ago greeted the dawn; now the chickens greet their breakfast with happy commotion. The valley is bathed in golden hues; dew sparkles on the vines.

But the sound of gunfire is closer than it has ever been. The few remaining defenders have fallen back to their final position—a barricade, blocking the entrance to Medjugorje. Not even the largest tank can force its way through this mass of welded steel I-beams; anyone entering Medjugorje will do so on foot.

The defenders are local men, known to many pilgrims. They were the ones pitching hay onto wagons at dawn, or driving a load of feed, or framing the new doors to the church—the ones who laid aside their tools in time to be at the rosary before late afternoon Mass.

Rosaries are around their necks now, as they fight with quiet heroism to prevent the enemy from reaching their families. But there are too many brown uniforms arrayed against them. The sun glints off their helmets, as they swarm like beetles through the trees to surround them. They will not rush the barricade, as long as its defenders are alive. But only a few still return fire, and there is no one to bring them more ammunition.

On the sun-drenched plaza before the church, the refugees are congregating for morning prayer. The air above them shimmers—their guardian angels are waiting to escort their souls to heaven. Moving among them are the villagers, helping in any way they can. There is the grandmother and grandson who used to stand by the path through the field, offering pieces of fruit to pilgrims who passed. There is the gap-toothed old man who was always so delighted when pilgrims came to stay with him. There is the ancient woman all in black who insisted in giving up her seat at the end of her pew to pilgrims—and in so doing touched hearts more profoundly than any sermon ever could.

There they all are—the old farmers, the mothers, children—doing what the *Gospa* has asked of them, ever since she first came: caring for the pilgrims selflessly, that they might see her Son in them. These refugees are the pilgrims now. And they can see Jesus in the villagers. Their fears are calmed.

In the distance, the gunfire lessens. Only a few more shots, then silence—until they hear the sounds of the beetle-men rushing towards them. . . .

What happens next, the reader can imagine as readily as the author. Keep in mind that it is what could happen— not what *has* to happen. If we will pray, we can alter that script, change the ending. That blissful, sparkling dawn can be followed by a scene of throngs of pilgrims like you and me, cheerfully congregating in the sun on the steps of St. James—or quietly queuing up at one of the confessionals, to cleanse our souls and start the beginning of the rest of our lives.

Which ending do you prefer? The outcome is in our hands.

24

The Thistle

Up on Podbrdo, not far from where the Gospa first appeared, a lone thistle grows. Half-hidden by rocks and shrubs, it has done well in this harsh and forbidding soil. It is a hardy little flower, its lavender bloom is iridescent in the setting sun.

The rose is the bloom most often associated with the Blessed Mother, but here in this severe mountain setting, the thistle seems singularly appropriate. In a way, it represents the faith of the people below—it does not need much rain; it can withstand the cruellest elements. It thrives on adversity. But at the same time, it is defenseless; it can be easily crushed by a single careless footstep—or the heel of a combat boot.

People coming up here to pray have noted it and smiled—and a few have smiled the more, realizing that God planted it there for the enjoyment of His children, and that He takes delight in their delight.

If the village below is to be devastated, if all of its inhabitants are to be slain, this thistle will still be here. And the light from their iridescent faith will continue to emanate from this place. It shines on in too many places, too many hearts now, for the darkness to ever overwhelm it.

Regardless of how the story ends, the light will have the victory. And this will be its final message: the witness of this place—of all that God has done here, in and through its people, and in and through the pilgrims whose hearts joined His here—will shine like a city set upon a hill. Medjugorje will live, as long as men pray and remember.

Printed by Paraclete Press
P. O. Box 1568
Orleans, MA 02653
1-800-451-5006